A Felon's Guide to Financial Recovery

GET OUT AND STAY OUT!

Robert E. Barth

Henry Lyon Books
FULTON, KY

Copyright © 2020 by GHE Publishing, LLC.

All rights reserved. No part of this publication may be reproduced, distributed or transmitted in any form or by any means, including photocopying, recording, or other electronic or mechanical methods, without the prior written permission of the publisher, except in the case of brief quotations embodied in critical reviews and certain other noncommercial uses permitted by copyright law.

Published by GHE Publishing LLC in cooperation with
  Henry Lyon Books
  an imprint of Master Design Publishing, LLC
  HenryLyonBooks.com

Cover and interior design by Faithe Thomas
Photos/Images © DepositPhotos.com

Ordering Information:
Special discounts are available on quantity purchases by corporations, associations, and others. For details, contact GHE Publishing (see info in back of book).

This publication is designed to provide best efforts for accurate and authoritative information with regard to the subject matter covered. Much of which the author has experienced himself personally. It is sold with the understanding that this is a self help design and if financial advice or other expert assistance is required, the services of a competent professional should be sought.

Print ISBN: 978-1-947482-22-7
Ebook ISBN:978-1-947482-23-4
Printed in the USA

Contents

Foreword vii
Acknowledgments xi
1. The Destination 1
2. Why People Fail Financially 21
3. Establishing Goals and Objectives 53
4. Establishing Your Current Status 81
5. Creating Your Personal
    Roadmap to Success 109
6. Pre-Release Plan Implementation 151
7. Post Release & Plan Implementation 159
8. Employment vs Self-Employment 185
9. Purchasing a Home for Little or No
    Money Down 203
10. Asset Protection Strategies 227
11. Arming Yourself for the Casino 235
12. Consider a New Life in a New State or
    Even a New Country 259
13. In California Expect the Unexpected 273

A Few Parting Shots 275
Money and the Mind? 281
The 30 Day Chart! 285
God-Health-Everything Else 287

*Dedication to
My Children to Whom
My Love Has No Bounds*

Robert

Taylor

Symphony

Allegra

Foreword

I am delighted and honored to have been asked to write the forward to Robert Barth's *A Felon's Guide to Financial Recovery*. Not only is the author a dear, personal friend, but he also has, in my view, the skillset and experience to deal with the challenges we face as felons or former felons in our society and the business community.

Robert has been self-employed for over forty years. He owned a chain of retail camera stores, a photo processing manufacturing plant, and a wholesale distribution company selling cameras, film, and related accessories and services. His skill set is unique in many ways, but I'd like to name two. When felons are released, many are challenged to obtain work. In many cases, individuals are better served by being in their own business. Robert's book can help guide you into your own business with the best chances of success. For those seeking employment, his current personal experiences, and his experience as an employer can not only help you find a job but a job that's well-matched to meet your personal financial goals and objectives.

ROBERT'S PROFESSIONAL CREDENTIALS:

Robert is a twenty-five year former veteran Certified Financial Planner, a twenty-year plus former California Real Estate Broker, and a twenty-five year former veteran Federal and State Tax Planner and Consultant. His credentials and experience will guide you through a very well organized process that will help you establish realistic goals and objectives and build a reliable roadmap to financial success.

This book is not one of those "get you pumped up, look at me: I am great, do what I tell you or you're not" smart books. It is just the opposite — Robert walks the talk. He knows the dark side first hand. He was arrested in 2011 for financial white-collar crimes. He was out on bail for almost three years, took his case to court (lost), and was sentenced to a term of nine years and four months. He spent four months in the Orange County Jail, five months in Wasco State Prison Reception, twenty-eight months in a state-run conservation camp (Fire Camp), and five months in the Sierra Conservation Center (Jamestown State Prison). He was released and paroled early because of his good behavior.

I was fortunate to meet Robert in the kitchen of Miramonte Fire Camp (CC#5). We worked together for over a year, twelve hours a day, seven days a week. He was always willing to share his knowledge and experience. By doing so, he has changed my life and changed the lives of so many other inmates throughout the system.

During November 2016, as a Christmas gift to the kitchen crew, he offered a series of unofficial workshops in the chow hall after dinner. He called the series: How to Prepare Financially For Your Release. Wow. Needless to say, the workshops were a major success. Then someone suggested the idea of combining the lessons into an interactive workbook for inmates. Then someone suggested the title to be *A Felon's Guide to Financial Recovery* and—here it is. It was planned and designed and partially written while Robert was in custody. The book could have been written entirely while in custody, but as you may or may not be aware, access to word processing equipment is almost impossible.

Being in custody can be either a curse or a blessing depending mainly on how one interprets his or her situation. For some, being arrested gives them a bed to sleep at night and three square meals a day. On the other end of the spectrum are business owners and executives who have stretched the rules to the point of criminal activities -victims in many cases of a weak economy or other economic circumstances.

Regardless of what category you fall into, an opportunity awaits you! Rather than spending your time drawing or tracing pictures, being a tattoo artist or recipient, making jewelry out of plastic bags, making pen or pencil holders, or designing the next gourmet food concept using a Ramen "Soup," you can prepare yourself with enough financial and life planning knowledge to change your life.

There's better news: this workbook applies to everyone in custody. So no matter if you're in county jail, on a county farm, in state prison reception, in state prison, in Federal prison, on a state or federal conservation camp, alternative Sentenced or on parole or probation, the one thing you will have plenty of is time. So no matter what form of custody you're currently in, by applying these principles, you can get ready to get out and stay out.

A Felon's Guide to Financial Recovery is about taking a journey—a journey to live a long, clean, healthy, and honest life. I'm blessed and thankful to the Lord our God every day for the opportunity He has given me to have met Robert and to be a part of this great project.

I am privileged and blessed.
Enjoy the Ride!

Anthony Mazziliano
GHE Publishing LLC Managing Member

Acknowledgments

Nothing ever is a solo event. There are books, schools, and Individuals who have inspired me over the years, and the following list in no way covers them all:
- The College for Financial Planning
- Steven Covey's *7 Habits,*
- Dr. J. Vernon McGee's *Thru the Bible* ministry and radio program
- Rabbi Nachman of Breslev's *The Empty Chair*
- Alan Morinis' *Everyday Holiness*
- John Tesh and
- Brian Tracy's *The Psychology of Achievement*

These influencers imparted concepts and belief systems that I've read and studied over the years, which are interwoven throughout this book.

Structurally, this book would not exist without the editing and designing skills of Faithe Thomas, whose guidance personified confidence and support in every aspect of this project. She literally made it happen.

Then there are those I met in custody on both sides of the fence. There are too many to list every one. For the boys dressed in Orange, let me acknowledge Jason Mayhall, who always said, "Never Give Up." Also, my kitchen companions: The Baker Erick

"Dub" Ellerbrock and Morris "Moe" Lotonuu, formally known as Morris Mulifai, the Burrito Master. On the Green Side, there was CDCR Sergeant Pablo Martinez, CDCR Officers Jack German, JJ Garrison, Bart Bauer, David Brisson, and Mozart Lozano.

Lastly, but most importantly, I am grateful for Rabbi Robin Foonberg, bless her soul, who stood up for me in court and stood by me through all the good and all the bad, and guided me back to the good.

Robert E. Barth

The Lord's Prayer:

Our Father Who art in heaven
hallowed be Thy name.
Thy kingdom come.
Thy will be done, on earth as it is in heaven.
Give us this day our daily bread.
And forgive us our trespasses,
as we forgive those who trespass against us.
And lead us not into temptation,
but deliver us from evil.
For Thine is the kingdom, the power, and the glory,
for ever and ever.

Amen.

CHAPTER 1

The Destination

> Don't make the same mistake as all those people who give up trying to change because they feel stuck in their habits. If you truly want to and are willing to work hard enough, you can overcome them.

Every journey has a destination, and this workbook is no different. Our goal is simple: Working together, we hope and pray that you will create a well-defined, personal life and financial plan specific to your situation. And then, upon your release, with this plan in place and a set of implementation instructions, you will have an action list of to do's and pretty much know what to do every day. It's certainly a structured approach, but what I have experienced first hand is that the longer you are in custody, the mind seems to slow down. It needs time to catch up in real-time. It does not happen overnight. Depending upon your age, it can take weeks, months, or years. So preparing and planning your own structured list of things to do, makes it less taxing on the brain. This, in turn, creates fewer mistakes (and you will make them—we are only human). The good news is that you will keep moving forward. And that will give you the best chance of success. The overall objective of this journey is to get out and stay out of custody forever.

Let me share this with you upfront: this is a very personal process, and it will not apply to anyone but yourself. Even if you think your friend, Bunkie or Cellie is in the same situation, they're not. So try to avoid getting into politics with this book. Everyone has their own set of circumstances, legal restrictions, family makeup, and personal issues. When you have created your plan and list of things to do, it's all you. Someone else following what you do could really put them in a bad situation. Your plan is your plan, and your Cellie's plan is theirs. There is one exception, while in custody, I ran across several inmates who could not read. They were embarrassed by it and were not upfront about it and did everything possible to hide the truth. If per chance your Bunkie or Cellie cannot read, after you complete the process for yourself, it would be a blessing for you to read to him or her and help them develop their plan.

Remember: *A Felon's Guide* was not designed to address everything that has ever happened to you in the past, the past that brought you to this point in your life. This book is about learning how to take charge, make changes, and move forward. It's a self-help book to change *your* future. Together we will be covering a lot of information. This process will, hopefully, make you aware of all the resources you have and things you should be doing right now to get started. Yes, right now! We are doing this way before your release because you can. And you have the time. There are lots of things you can do to be better prepared. Don't concern yourself with who's making the next spread for dinner, start tonight by taking a few minutes after lights out and pray to God and ask Him for help in your own words and begin with visualizing your new life — a new life of happiness, prosperity, success, and personal transformation.

Have you ever been stressed out over having to make a financial decision? For most of us, the answer is "yes." Why is there so much stress? Not that stress is a bad thing. If it can keep you sharp and help you to be more focused during a financial transaction, it could be a very good thing. But for most of us, especially many that I have met while being in custody, the stress level involved in making financial decisions is actually debilitating to the point that their comprehension was challenged. In most cases, the level of stress caused those involved with making financial decisions mentally handicapped. It was almost impossible to think clearly. Rather than making an informed decision, it became more like a gamble. An internal voice inside their head was saying, "I hope, I hope, I hope I'm making the right decision." There are lots of reasons for this, and we will be illustrating them in detail in the next chapter appropriately titled "Why do people fail financially."

Here's a really cool question: Do you know how to make the right financial decision? Or how about this question: What if you knew that your financial decision was the absolute best decision for your situation? Would you not be less stressed out? And if you knew that this was absolutely the right thing to do, wouldn't it give you more confidence to move on to bigger and better things? I'd like you to realize that there are correct answers to specific personal financial questions. Questions like, How much car should I buy? How much house? Should I rent? Should I buy? How much insurance should I purchase? Am I making enough money? That's just a beginning sample. There are exact answers to all kinds of financial questions, and if you keep reading, you will learn the process and say what most people say: it all makes just total common sense. Because it is.

Let me also mention that in the course of being a Certified Financial Planner 20 plus years, many of my clients have often felt a little inadequate and think, "Why didn't I think of that?" Forget it and drop the drama. It just doesn't matter. What matters is that you took a shot and pulled the trigger to read this book in an attempt to change your life. Take your time reading this book—there's no rush. If you don't get a concept, go back and read it again. It's all good. That feeling of "Why didn't I think of that?" doesn't just apply to people who are starting over.

Over 95% of Americans are financially uneducated. I'm talking multi-millionaires—people who you thought knew everything just because they have accumulated some wealth. But let me also share that in the course of being an elite financial planner, I met plenty of folks with lots of money. Most of them either inherited it or won a big law suit. Not many earned it. But the ones that earned it, many of them like you, who started over from scratch, were some of the most dynamic people I have ever met. They benefited not just their company but their community. These success stories become the leaders of their communities and have the biggest heart to help others. There is a word that separates the ones who have earned their wealth on their own from the rest of us — and that word is "THANKFUL." Remember that, not to lose my thoughts here, most people share that feeling of "Why didn't I think of that." That's the value of having outside objective advice. So no worries about feeling inadequate. Be THANKFUL for the helpful, professional advice.

Next, you need to be mentally prepared for success. You may think that's totally crazy, but it's not, it's a lot easier to manage nothing. Cause when you have nothing, there's nothing to think about. When you see an advertisement for a new car, you think, "I can't afford it." When you see the new cell phone, you think, "I can't afford it." But once you can afford it, now you start thinking and asking yourself which one is the best. You start paying attention to all the competitive products. Then you start doing research, start checking all the pricing, and listen to the comments from people who have purchased and used the product. It takes energy, a lot of energy! It takes a lot of energy to make money and, more importantly, a lot of energy to keep it. I wish I had a dollar for every time I told a client it's not what you make that matters most— it's what you keep. How many of us know or knew someone who was rolling in the dough, only to squander their money, go broke, and have to start all over again? There are so many distractions, so many advertisements that bombard you from the moment you awake. Christmas, Prime Day, Cyber Monday, Black Friday, all the public holidays, Tax-Free weekends—and then there's the opponent. Do not underestimate **The Power of The Opponent.** The opponent can make you befriend people for all the wrong reasons. The opponent wants you seeking quick pleasures rather than long term happiness. And the opponent wants you to believe in fantasy lifestyles that are promoted on television, radio, and the internet. The opponent constantly bombards you, and there is no escape. You can't run away from the opponent because the opponent is you and your own ego.

Many of us have found ourselves in custody because we just had to have it, even if it was illegal. That is where spirituality and faith in God can give you a solid foundation to feel thankful for what you do have and the ability to change your ways. Being more spiritually aware can help you recognize when the opponent starts taking over. Prayer and being thankful to the Almighty will give you the strength to defeat that opponent and allow you to build personal and spiritual strength. That strength will then enable you to establish a fundamental foundation for dealing with success. You will be able to make money and build your wealth— and more importantly, you will be able to keep it!

Getting back to what we were just discussing... So, why does it seem like all financial decisions are so complicated? The answer is simple: Money! And the more complicated the professionals make it, the more you will need them. It's very self-serving. There's nothing wrong with professional advice, but let's face it, most financial advisers are not familiar with the unique set of circumstances that a felon has to deal with. Professional advisers also prefer to deal with affluent clients (because they can pay more) and charge big fees and commissions. It doesn't make sense sometimes, but banks lend money to people who have money and not to people who don't, but who really need it more. Although choosing where to bank is not like choosing which grocery store to shop at, but it's really not that far away. Let's start by saying that the best financial decisions are made when you personally understand them and are in consideration of six things.

> If you have no goals you will be bored: you will be unhappy because you are empty.
>
> Alfred Armand Montapert

All Personal Financial Planning decisions fall into six understandable disciplines. And since most of us don't like the sound of the word discipline, let's just say they fall into one of six financial boxes or areas.

They are:
- Cash Flow Planning / Cash Management
- Risk Management
- Investment Planning
- Tax Planning
- Longer Range / Retirement Planning
- Estate Planning

As you see from the illustration on the next page, they are all interrelated, interconnected. Now let's discuss each one and make some common sense on how this interrelationship works. For example: Let's buy a home.

You would need to know how much house you can afford. That process is called **Cash Flow Planning**.

How will you protect that home and the property held in that home? That process is called **Risk Planning or Risk Management**.

Does the home purchase have tax advantages? That's **Tax Planning**.

Are you and your family suitable for this real estate based asset investment and what is its expected return? That's **Investment Planning**.

Does this home purchase bring you closer to or further away from you and your family's future goals/retirement goals? That's **Longer Range Planning** also known as **Retirement Planning**.

How will you title this home: your name or joint names? And if you unexpectedly passed away, who would you leave it to? That's **Estate Planning**.

Having these ducks in order makes this home purchase logical, affordable, and done with a level of confidence, which can make the process enjoyable even though challenging, involving, and focused. It's the complete opposite of "What have I gotten myself into?" And you won't become disabled over the stress. The important thing is to see the interrelationship. It's a lot more than thinking you can afford a home because you have so much in the bank or you make so much per week. Or the best one is *asking the real estate agent* if you can afford a home. Now there's an unbiased opinion! NOT! You need to know if you can afford the home.

Here's another way we can narrate the interrelationships. If you have more money coming in than going out, you have a positive cash flow (Cash Flow Planning). And it's worth something and, therefore, a very valuable asset that needs to be protected (Risk Planning). When you're making money, you will be paying taxes (Tax Planning). And if you have money left over after paying your taxes, you will have money for savings and investment (Investment Planning). With a positive, protected cash flow, after paying your taxes, and putting enough money aside for your savings and investment needs, you can start thinking about future plans such as retirement, another home, or children's education (Future Planning).

Some practicing professionals call this retirement planning, but it's really much more than that. Lastly, if you've done a good job in these five areas upon your death, you will have accumulated wealth— the remainder of which could be left to family, friends, or a good charitable cause (Estate Planning).

This is the total scope of personal financial planning. All of the components are important. Still, for this book, our purpose will be mainly focused on cash flow planning and risk management planning. I've also included several special topics: *Creative Home Acquisition: How to acquire a home for little or no money out of pocket*, *The Tax Benefits of Owning Your Own Company*, and *Money Management System for Playing Certain Casino games*.

I struggled with putting in the Casino aspect. Years ago, when I was a much younger man, living in New York, if you wanted to go gambling, you had to fly to Las Vegas. So it was always a major planned trip. But today there are casinos everywhere, and they are so enticing. So I said to myself, "Self, if we are trying to build wealth and stay out of custody why not teach a strategy so that when they decide to go (and you will be going, let's be realistic), they will have a fighting chance to win and not alter their lifestyle." In fact, I asked several fellow inmates ready to be released who was picking them up. So many times the answer is "My wife" or "My girlfriend" "... and we are going to the hotel casino to catch up on lost time." So I decided to share the system. With just a little luck, you will stand a fighting chance of coming home with some money and not licking your wounds and having to alter your financial plan. Plus you can buy playing cards! They are readily available at every level of custody, and you will have plenty of time to practice and master your casino skills. You can even practice and play by yourself acting as both dealer and player. It's time to take a break from pinochle and spades.

So that's it. Six areas. For the most part, in this book, we will spend our time in primarily two areas for now. These areas are cash flow and risk management, which are the real focus of this workbook. We'll be touching on the other four financial areas, but those will become more important several months down the road.

> Know! A person walks in life on a very narrow bridge. The most important thing is not to be afraid.
>
> Rebbe Nachman of Breslov

A Six Step Planning Process

Now that you know the scope of the book, let's discuss the process the professionals use to achieve personal financial goals and objectives. By the way, you can use the same process to achieve non-financial goals as well. I spent many years in business learning how to accomplish goals. I was obsessed with it. So much so, that one day, as I was listening to a cassette tape in my car on the way to the office, a gentleman by the name of Brian Tracy shared a brand new concept called a "to-do list." Yep, this was a brand new concept back in the '70s: write down what you wanted to get done for the day, week, or month on a sheet of paper and then start to do them. Once you completed a task, check it off. Before that, most people were carrying around their to-do list in their head. I was so impressed with this revelation that I purchased plane tickets for all the key employees of the company and flew everyone from New York to Boston to participate in an educational seminar on improving productivity in our Photo Processing Laboratory and Retail Locations. Little did I realize that it was Brian Tracy himself who taught every key employee of my company the value of planning and creating to-do lists. That simple process required everyone to pre-think. You had to sit down, think of what you wanted to get done, figure out where, how, and why. Then you had to write it down before you started to get it done.

At the time, we never realized that the man standing in front of us would go on to become a superstar. From Wikipedia: Brian Tracy is a Canadian-American motivational public speaker and self-development author. He is the author of over seventy books that have been translated into dozens of languages. His popular books are Earn What You're Really Worth, Eat That Frog!, and The Psychology of Achievement." When I attended the College for Financial Planning in the '90s, they educated me much more formally on basically the same processes, just much more expanded. The Financial planning process is a precise process for achieving targeted financial goals. But it can be used universally. It will also help you to develop a realistic, implementable plan (The To-do List). Why so much fuss about creating a plan? Because people are not superhuman. Most people can not juggle six things at once. Having a plan, a set of blueprints, right in front of your eyes can help you see a bigger picture. The fact that it's written down and in front of your eyes allows you to make changes in advance, rather than doing the "oops we goofed." Plus, you get a chance to study the changes and see how those changes impacted the entire project. And all of this even before you actually do it. That is pretty cool stuff. The following are the formal six-step process to create that set of financial blueprints.

The Financial Planning Process

Step 1

Gather Information

There is a need to take the time to collect basic personal data. Name, address, age, family, criminal history, charges, and sentence information. Then clarify your present situation by collecting and assessing all relevant financial data such as lists of assets and liabilities, tax returns, records of securities transactions, insurance policies, wills, pension plans, etc. Some of these items you have locked up in your head, in your locker, in boxes or folders. Most of you **do not** have much, so let's put in a little creative energy here and use what you have and your best guess. You should be able to get the criminal files from the institution. It may take a bit of work, but it can and should be done.

Step 2

Identify Financial Goals

This is by far the most critical step in the process: defining and developing realistic goals and objectives. It is also the most vital part of the process. (You need to forget that song "I want to be a Billionaire, so Freakin bad.") Build a list of realistic personal goals, realistic financial goals, goals specifically devoted to your family and friends, and lastly, but most importantly, your spiritual goals. Do your best to start thinking about your financial and personal values and attitudes. These may include providing for children's education, supporting elderly parents, or relieving immediate financial pressures. Keep a note pad by your rack. If you wake up in the middle of the night with an idea, write it down.

Step 3

Identify Financial Problems

You need to come to grips with where you are financially right now. In custody, this can be quite uncomfortable, but it still needs to be done. You will need all the facts to establish your current status. Then we are going to view them from two different points of view. We are going to take a quick snapshot of your finances: " the freeze-frame view." Then we will take a "motion picture view." The combination of both should give you a really good picture of just where you are financially right now. Issues will start to surface, and most of the time, it won't make you feel very good. The reason is that these financial problems appear as a barrier to achieving financial success. Your cash flow may be inadequate, or the current investments may not be winning the battle with the changing economic times. You may not have any money or assets at all. Plus, we have a bunch of common felon-based problem areas that must be identified before solutions can be found—issues like restitution, child support, back taxes, and personal and family obligations. The good news is this book is going to help you deal with them, but even better is that you are identifying them. We want to avoid surprises.

STEP 4

Create Your Financial Plan

You are going to create and write your own personal financial plan with three earmarked points in time. The first point is from the day you first step out of the gates to freedom up to around the six-month mark. The second earmark is from six months to eighteen months. And the last earmark is from eighteen months to thirty-six months and beyond. Don't worry, there's enough information to help you start thinking about solutions and alternative solutions. Plus, I do plan on providing either live or on-line to help.

Step 5

Implement Strategies

It may sound crazy, but a lot of people create great plans, write them out slowly and carefully, with great penmanship, but never put them into use. We want to create a set of step-by-step, written instructions to get the job done. We will be using some organizational and time management skills that will be needed to get this project rolling. **Then we will create the daily To-Do list.** Many of those To-Do things you can get started on right now! While in custody! It surprises most people. You're doing time, why not put that time to good use.

Step 6

Monitor and Review

It is essential to take the time to review your plan, celebrate your achievements, and make adjustments to the things that you're having a hard time with. Situations are continually changing in and out of custody all the time. Life is just not a ratchet, financial and life plans need to be fluid and ever-changing. At each earmark, 6 months, 18 months, and 36 months, it is very important to review what worked and make revisions to the items that did not work. This way, you can be sure that you are moving in the right direction to achieve your goals. The first year of freedom should be the most dramatic as far as change is concerned. In my personal journey, I walked out of Jamestown with $200, and within a year, I was looking to purchase a home. Yes, everyone's situation is different. Still, I can tell you this, I prayed every day, sometimes in the morning and sometimes at night and sometimes all day long. I'm convinced the Lord has shined His great light upon me, and I am very thankful and blessed for it. Once you're past the 36-month mark, your financial situation should be re-assessed at least annually to account for changes in your life and current economic conditions.

> If you believe that you can damage, then believe you can fix. If you believe that you can harm, then believe that you can heal.
>
> Rebbe Nachman of Breslov

CHAPTER 2

Why People Fail Financially

So you've made a mistake, a big mistake, a mistake that has cost you your freedom. Now you have a new tag line, "A Felon". You're now in custody awaiting trial or serving your sentence. I say, "Let the lawyers do their thing." It's time to start laying out the groundwork for changing your life and moving forward to financial recovery, permanent freedom, and eventual success. But before we do that, let's take a step back to examine and ask yourself, "Why are you here?" Only you know that answer, and it's worth it to do a little soul searching. For me, with no uncertain terms, it was **Lack of Faith.** The opponent, "My Ego," was in charge. I did not believe that God would provide. I lacked patience. I lacked honesty. I lacked charity. I lacked trust. I lacked gratitude. I lacked tranquility. I Lacked kindness. I lacked truth, enthusiasm, humility, order, honor, and generosity. That is a big mouthful, but at the heart and soul of all those fantastic human character traits listed above is one very simple word: "God." You must, with all your heart and soul, believe God is there for you. Then you'll realize that you are not in control of everything. God, your Creator, is and, in fact, He is in complete control of everything that happens to you - even things that seem insignificant. Nothing in your life can change for the better or worse unless God wants it. That, by all means, does not mean you can lay down on your rack and do nothing. It means your attitude towards Him and awareness needs to rise to the occasion.

> When your own world is fractured, increase your knowledge of God. It will spawn inner peace. When the outside world is fractured, promote the search for truth. It will spawn universal peace.
>
> Rebbe Nachman of Breslov

Throughout the book I will share some of the wisdom from some of the world's most renowned wise men of faith. Open your hearts and minds and try to elevate yourself to a new level of spirituality, thinking, and awareness.

So Why Do People Fail Financially?

Reason #1 - No Goals

Most, if not all, financial professionals agree that the leading reason for financial failure is just simply not having any financial goals. Or, if they do have goals, they are totally unrealistic. Like the song says, "Wanna be a Billionaire, So Freakin Bad." But the road to a healthy financial lifestyle is more like taking a road trip. It requires you to sit down, build a realistic road-trip, and not a trip to Mars. For example: if you're using Google Maps, the first question is: "choose a destination." That's even way, way before you get the best route to get you from point A to point B. The first thing you need to do is set those destinations, and those destinations are going to represent your goals and objectives. In general, most people fail in defining their financial destinations. What commonly occurs is "it's all go go go in life" and then suddenly you run out of cash, then run up a bunch of credit cards bills until you can't breathe anymore. And then you start thinking about making a budget or finding another job that helps pay off those credit cards. Some folks start thinking, I don't need to work harder, I'll just start complaining to the boss, start slacking off on the job, and then ask for a pow-wow with the boss — with the strategy "if you pay me more, I will work harder." Personally, as an employer, I loved that line! And my answer to this not-very-smart employee, who was trying to outsmart the boss, was really simple: "If you weren't giving me 110% to begin with, you don't deserve anything! Get back to work!" Think it doesn't happen? I made that speech 10 times every year!

Still having financial pressure? "The Opponent Can Arrive." (The opponent is your ego.) I like to think of The Opponent as Darth Vader from the Dark Side. The Dark Side kicks in, and you start thinking about stealing, selling drugs, or doing some other criminal act to get what you need. **Let's get real serious here, no bullshit, most of you are probably in custody for just that reason.** Without planning and living beyond your means, life eventually catches up, and you make poor decisions. In a lot of cases, all of this mess could have been avoided in the first place, simply by thinking about your financial destination in advance.

One more classic example of not thinking about financial issues in advance that happens to so many is what I call **Tax Bite**. Your tax return is due, and you **"Ouch!"** owe money, and *now* you start thinking of ways to reduce taxes. You don't lower taxes at the end of the year, you reduce taxes by planning it out from the beginning of the year or even sooner than that. Reactivity in the real world just doesn't work. You need to establish realistic goals and objectives proactively in advance. "It's not that financial plans fail, it's that people fail to plan!" And way before even having a plan, you need a destination to begin the process.

This is an essential concept worthy of an example because people put a lot of time into making travel plans and zero time when it comes to making financial plans. I'm thinking the reason is that it is a lot more fun to plan a trip than think about money. Regardless let's look at an example: Let's say we are in Los Angeles, and we are planning to take a trip to San Francisco. First things first. We now have a destination: San Francisco is *our goal*. We can now move on to establishing the next step: our *current status*. How many people will be traveling? How much money do we have to spend? And how long do we plan on staying? These answers are our *current status*. With those ingredients, we can now *develop the plan*. We can now decide on the vehicle we should use: Auto, Truck, Van, Bus, Plane or Boat. We can decide on what route you want to take: West-Coast Waterway, Pacific Coast Highway, The 5 Freeway, The 101 Freeway, Long Beach Airport, LAX, or other airports. If driving, we can choose to drive at very high speed, get there really fast, and take a lot of risks. Or we can be too safe and drive real slow and take forever to get there. Or we can find the sweet spot in the middle, the speed that gets us there most efficiently, safely, and on time. We want the sweet spot, and the planning process does just that. Because the same logic can be applied to obtaining financial goals and objectives, and if we are a little lucky in this process, maybe, just maybe, you can find planning your financial success even more enjoyable than taking a trip to San Francisco.

Think about this, how crazy would it be if we just got in the car and just drove? We'd spend a lot of gas and time going nowhere. Or what about planning a trip to Mars? This kind of thinking has to stop right now. A good portion of this book is dedicated to creating, defining, and thinking about realistic financial and non-financial goals and objectives. Those goals and objectives are your destination. Once you have that destination, you can start the process of figuring out how to get there, but without it, you're just going nowhere.

Determining realistic goals and objectives is the most important step to reaching your destinations. Start asking yourself, "What are your financial goals?" Write them down. We will be exploring them in detail a bit later. Suggestion* It's an excellent idea to keep a note pad handy near your rack just in case you start getting some good ideas. Carry them around if need be, but write them down so you can refer to them later. Let's continue on with why people financially fail.

REASON #2 - LACK OF GENERAL FINANCIAL KNOWLEDGE

It's nobody's fault. General knowledge like buying a house, a car, insurance, etc. and knowing and understanding all your real financial assets don't come easy. Our public schools do very little to prepare you for real life. I'm not belittling the high school system, but when was the last time you saw a high school class entitled *How to purchase an automobile*? What about: *How to purchase a home*? *How to buy auto insurance*? *What's the difference between Savings and Investing*? *Learning about your credit score*? I didn't think you had! But students do spend a lot of time learning about triangles and algebra — "real exciting stuff." In the real world, you're expected to learn from your parents or the person who is selling these products and services to you. For many of you in custody, you didn't have much in the way of parental guidance, and so now you're supposed to trust that person selling you your house or your car or whatever. Think about this, for most people, the biggest investment purchase for their entire life is purchasing a home. Yet, we are expected to rely on the real estate salesperson who has a commission at stake for their objective advice? Nothing against real estate people, but you should have at least the basic knowledge in your pocket before dealing with these professionals. Doing this on complete faith and trust with some of these professionals is sometimes called "learning the hard way." You are the one with the cash, and the professional is supposed to be the one with the experience. But sometimes, at the end of some of these deals, the professionals are the ones with the cash, and you are the one with the experience.

At the beginning of this book, we discussed that the level of stress dealing with financial issues can elevate to the point of disability. That stress is a real deal because so many people are faced with so many unknowns. So it's worth your while to use your time wisely in custody and self educate, quietly to yourself on your rack. There are plenty of books written on financial subjects. If you are out on probation or parole, look into the Saddleback Church Financial Coaching/Workshops, or the GHE Publishing Website. You want places that can provide useful objective financial information. Get all the information you can, do your part and study the information to the best of your ability and then have faith in the Lord. Trust God. He is here to provide. He wants to provide for all your needs. All you need to do is ask, and the best way to ask God for something is through prayer. But you need to put in the effort. You put in the effort, then cast your burden upon His shoulders and let God do the rest.

Reason #3 - Misunderstanding the Value of Compound Interest

"I'm starting from scratch. It's impossible!" That kind of thinking is a major roadblock to financial success. You need to have some faith. Building wealth is like spiritual development; it's not a get rich quick scheme. It is a slow continuous process. Just like spiritual growth, you need to grow carefully:

Spiritual growth and character growth must proceed slowly and steadily. Too often, we want to improve ourselves and our relationships so quickly that we make ourselves frustrated and confused. Gifted sports stars, actors, musicians and superstars, those born into wealth by inheritance, those who won the lottery and those who won the big lawsuit, all have one thing in common. They are rare! That's why they are constantly stalked by the media. And even with all their wealth, if they lack a spiritual foundation, they live very unhappy lives. The reason? They start to worship their money rather than God. People can become so focused on exterior pleasures and material items they lose sight of real happiness that is internal.

So, unless you fit in one of those extraordinary superstar groups, you will be accumulating wealth just like the rest of us mortals— the way you should— by building your wealth slowly and steadily. The good news is that even with a slow and steady approach, understanding compound interest really helps you stay focused. You can easily calculate your future results today and see the bright lights shining at the end of the success tunnel. Why? Because little pieces of money saved over long periods of time can build substantial wealth, very realistically— making it very obtainable.

As an illustration, let me offer you a job. This job will pay you one dollar for the first day, two dollars for the second, four dollars for the third, and so on for thirty days. Would you take that job? **Yes!** Most people jump up in my class and say yes. And when I ask them why they tell me because it's a lot of money. Then I ask how much money do you think it is at the end of 30 days? They say a million dollars, but they never say over a half a billion dollars! On the back page of this book, I give you the entire 30 day schedule. The amount is a staggering $536,870,912.00! That's *FIVE HUNDRED AND THIRTY-SIX MILLION EIGHT HUNDRED SEVENTY THOUSAND NINE HUNDRED TWELVE DOLLARS!* Get out your calculator or do the math by hand. It doesn't matter. One dollar for the first day, two for the second, four for the third, and keep going. The example is used to illustrate that most people just can not comprehend the value of compounding interest. But with proper planning, combined with the discipline of saving small amounts of money over long periods of time, you can and will build significant wealth. You can pre-calculate the amount by using any future value calculator (and there are hundreds of them for free online). If you have no access, ask a family member to help. You calculate the amount you plan on saving each month or week, then plug in the number of weeks, months, or years. You will see the results in advance. I recently did a calculation for a friend who was receiving $2000 a month from Social Security. He did not need the money. At his age (60), if he lived into his 90s (or 30 more years), he would be a billionaire.

The Key is maintaining and monitoring. *You Also Need A Positive Cash Flow, Then You Need To Earn A Reasonable Return On What You Saved.* If you're like most people seeing the end result will keep you motivated. Savings and Compound Interest is the opposite of the Dark Side. It's more like Luke Skywalker. "**Use the Force, Luke.**" You need it because everywhere, and every moment, someone from the Dark Side is trying to separate you from your money. You want to get to know the compounding of interest. Slow and steady wins the race; the quick fixes can put you back behind bars!

Reason #4 - Poor Investing

A better way to describe this would be that the chosen investments did not match up to the investor's needs. Now that may sound like a bunch of bull, but the fact of the matter is that once people finally accumulate enough money to invest (and that may take years), they go and make their financial decisions based upon some hot tip their neighbor gave them because the neighbor has a nicer car or lawnmower. The logic being that your neighbor really must know what they are doing, and he wouldn't lie to me since he lives right next door. But in reality, your neighbor is not you.

Let's not forget the "hot tip" on television. I mean, after all, if you are on TV you must be a super-duper financial professional. Let's just say that investing can be very complicated. The media plans it that way, and they feed your ego too—Your Opponent (Darth Vader from the Dark Side). There was an infomercial on late-night TV where this guy literally said, "If you come to my seminar, I will teach you how to be rich. If you don't, you're stupid." He said: "Look at me! I have beautiful women" (and you see several women in bikinis). He then said, "Look at my Rolls Royce," and then repeated the invitation to come to his seminar... because "If you don't, you're stupid."

Never do you need to be stronger with your faith and realize that there is no such thing as a hot tip or that attending some seminar will somehow make you rich overnight. It's just not going to happen. Investing is a carefully calculated and studied process that needs to be matched to your specific situation and risk tolerance, and no one else's. Here's some basic advice: "If you don't understand it, don't do it." I should also mention that if you're not comfortable with an investment, it's not worth it. We will not be going into much detail on investment planning in this book. Most of our readers need to focus on savings rather than investing, and there's a big difference. It will become clearer as you get more and more into the book.

So why do people lose so much of their wealth with poor investments? Well, for one, investing should only occur after you have accumulated enough savings. You should never be forced (with an emphasis on the word forced) to liquidate the investment prematurely. Also, the decision to make an investment needs to match up with your time horizon, return expectations, and your risk tolerance.

Let's use one practical example to bring this point home. Alan has a $100,000 Certificate of Deposit that came due and available to invest. Alan also found out that his neighbor has done really well in the stock market, specifically the S&P. Alan researches the Standard and Poor's index. It has historically returned 10% since its inception in 1914. Alan and his wife Robin and daughter Miriam are also planning to move and buy a new home, the neighbor is not. *That's a Big Deal.* The hot tip neighbor doesn't know what Alan's family plans are, what Alan and Robin's risk tolerance level is, nor that they are looking to move to a new school district.

Alan's money in the Certificate of Deposit took years to save up. But because of the Hot Tip neighbor, Alan opens up an online trading account. He even has the new App on his phone! Alan buys the stock representing the S&P Index SPDR S&P 500 ETF Trust (SPYDR) with the logic that he will be buying low and selling high. One year goes by, and he's up 8%! Doing pretty good. It's January, and Miriam is going to be in a new school district this fall. So Alan and Robin start aggressively looking for the house to purchase so that the family will be able to move before the summer and get Miriam registered for school. They find the home they want, but they need a $40,000 down payment and $10,000 for a variety of one-time moving expenses. The mortgage is already approved, pending their $40,000 down payment. Everything is going great. Then Alan wakes up Monday morning to hear that there's been a terrorist attack, and his portfolio is now worth $60,000! If he sells today, he will get $60,000.00, and if he doesn't, it may be worth $40,000.00 tomorrow. He freaks out. The wifey says they have to move now. Miriam is already registered for the new school. They have already signed the contracts. The escrow is open. And they are committed to the purchase and locked in or face a lawsuit.

They ended up selling and losing 40%. Why? Not because it was a poor investment. The S&P will eventually recover. But it was a poor investment decision guided by their ego. A classic investment mismatch: they had a short-term money need and parked their money in a long-term investment. Unless your day trading (SPYDR), you do it with long-term hold intentions of 5- 7 years minimum. The investment's time horizon did not match the need. In this case, when you are going to need the money in the short-term, don't worry about making money on the money. Forget the return, keep the money in cash, savings, or a money market fund. You just needed a safe place to hold it in anticipation of the home purchase. It just doesn't matter that Alan's neighbor chose S&P and did well. It's Alan and Robin's family's financial decision (The Family Had a Short Term Objective) to buy a new house. That should have been their focus. This type of investment mismatch happens all the time. *Your* Money, *Your* Goals!

REASON #5 - MISUNDERSTANDING OF OUR TAX LAWS

Federal Judge Learned Hand made the following famous quote, "Anyone may so arrange his affairs that his taxes shall be as low as possible; he or she is not bound to choose that pattern which will best pay the Treasury; there is not even a patriotic duty to increase one's taxes." (*Helvering v. Gregory*, 69 F.2d 809, 810-11 (2d Cir. 1934).) "Over and over again courts have said that there is nothing sinister in so arranging one's affairs as to keep taxes as low as possible. Everybody does so, rich or poor; and all do right, for nobody owes any public duty to pay more than the law demands: taxes are enforced exactions, not voluntary contributions. To demand more in the name of morals is mere cant." (*Commissioner v. Newman*, 159 F.2d 848, 851 (2d Cir. 1947) - dissenting opinion.)

Yet we see very little effort to reduce taxes **in advance of when taxes are due**. Attempting to do this at tax time (during preparation) is futile. Tax preparation is *not* tax planning. Tax planning is a major area of failure for most people. It is often overlooked and can change your lifestyle. Let me share a real-life story from one of my former clients (the names are changed to protect the innocent). It is the story of Gary and Susan— two public servants who were in their late 20's or early 30's. I mention that because professional financial planners mainly see an older crowd (the majority in their 40's, 50's and 60's). Gary was in law enforcement, and Susan was a school teacher. This couple was referred by another client, and I agreed to a complimentary consultation. During that consultation, they explained to me that they were into debt up to their eyeballs, that they wanted to start a family, and eventually that Susan would be a stay-at-home mom. I explained that this advice does not come cheap and that they may not get any short-term value in comparison to the planning fees I would charge. Gary shared that his father died broke; his mother lives in a trailer park; his brothers are up to their eyeballs in debt/broke; and that they all had one thing in common: they never did any financial planning. Gary said he didn't care that the cost may be greater than the reward now. He wanted to go through the process. If the advice was not helpful now, it would have value in the future. I couldn't argue with that.

As part of the process, I needed to gather accurate financial information about the clients' finances. Think about it: how can you make recommendations based on false data? It is critical to the process that we calculate all the money coming into the household and all the money going out of the household. So I calculated all of their income and all of their expenses and found a discrepancy of $10,000. In other words, I calculated all their yearly income and all their yearly expenses, and they were $10,000 short! Well, I started wondering if there was a mistake. I went over the numbers again and again. It certainly was not a mistake. I reviewed this with the clients, and both had absolutely nothing to say. Finally, I said, "Look, I'm gonna take a break and run and go to the men's room for a few minutes. When I return, I need to know what you're not telling me. If you don't, well, unfortunately, we are gonna have to end this relationship. We cannot build a financial plan on false or incorrect information."

I left the room thinking that there must be drugs, or another woman, or another man. It was getting crazy, and it was driving me crazy. What could it be? I walked back into the meeting room and found Gary's head hanging down. I thought, "Oh, boy, here it comes." Gary then proceeded to tell me about his garage. He has been moonlighting to make some extra money by fixing and painting people's cars. And he was restoring a vehicle which he purchased. He had been spending lots of money on the restoration and had not told Susan.

The restoration part was new, but the moonlighting has been going on for many years. Now that we got that out of the way, which was a major relief, I explained that I needed to postpone the meeting while I did some additional calculations. Additionally, I needed Gary's tax returns for the past three years. So to make a very long story a little shorter... as I suspected, he did not document any of the expenses or income on the autos he repaired. He had been running a repair business out of his garage for the past three years. He simply didn't know he could write off all the expenses related to that business. Because he was a police officer, he thought it best just to keep it quiet.

With the new information in hand, I made a tax recommendation to file amended returns for the past three years. We made sure to take deductions for the use of the garage, cell phones, office expenses, the new equipment that was purchased, depreciation of existing tools, paint, etc. These tax refunds were large enough to pay off all their credit card debt and loans. Gary's credit score went through the roof, and he was able to refinance his home to a lower interest rate, making smaller payments. Without those monthly credit card payments and with a lower mortgage payment, they finally had a substantial positive monthly cash flow. By the way, Gary eventually sold that house and made a considerable profit. He rolled the profit into a larger house and was able to start his own company. Susan was able to be a stay-at-home mother. They now have 5 children. There's a lot to learn here. First of all, you always need to provide accurate information to your advisor. And secondly, there are benefits to being in your own business (particularly in the area of taxes). You are not obligated to pay any more in taxes than what's legally required.

Below I created a chart to compare the same amount of money earned as an employee vs. as self-employed. Remember, this is 2017-2018 Tax law, and if there is anything I learned about taxes, it is that they are always changing. So either study the code while in custody or find a competent tax planner/preparer upon your release.

Here's what that looks like for an individual earning $100,000 as an employee, or the equivalent $107,650 as a 1099 contractor/self employed:

	W-2 Salary	**1099 Contractor or Self-Employed**
Gross Income	$100,000	$107,650
Social Security or Self-Employment Tax	($7,650)	($15,210)
SE Tax Deduction	$0	($7,605)
20% Pass-Through Deduction	$0	($17,608)
Standard Deduction	($12,000)	($12,000)
Taxable Income	$88,000	$70,436
Income Tax	($15,300)	($11,435)
After-Tax Income	**$77,051**	**$81,004**

Please take note of the term *Gross Income*. This is the result of all your business income *less* all of your business expenses. So, for instance, let's say you owned a mobile car detailing business, and your office was in your home (computer, internet, etc.). You used your cell phone as the means of contacting your customers and suppliers, and you used your van with all the detailing equipment to go to all the locations. All of these, in one way or another, are going to reduce that *Gross Income*.

When you're an employee, in most cases, your cell phone expenses will not be deductible. When you are in business for yourself and using it for your business, it will be deductible. Your home computer for personal use, in most cases, is not deductible. But when it is used for business, the computer and related expenses are all deductible from that *Gross Income*, and that lowers the *Taxable Income* number. The lower the *Taxable Income*, the lower your taxes will be. The area in your home (even if rented), which is used as office space, is deductible as a business expense, but not as an employee. And the list goes on and on. Go to a car detailing convention in Las Vegas at the Mirage Hotel, and the whole trip is deductible if you are self-employed. The key thing here is documentation. You must save everything for your tax preparer. There's nothing to explain; there's nothing to feel guilty about. This is the black and white tax law. There's nothing wrong with you going out to dinner with a prospective customer or supplier and enjoying dinner. As long as it's for a business purpose and documented, it's deductible. So unless you have a blessed job, paying lots of money and with lots of benefits, consider becoming self-employed or an independent contractor.

Lastly, most of you may have tax returns that have not been filed. DO NOT WORRY!!!!! The IRS, believe it or not, is a very open-minded group. Good faith and honesty go a long way here. The key thing is to communicate with them. It's not easy, but you must communicate. Share your story, and they will give you affordable alternatives—and they have lots of them. Then, just stay current on all the new stuff going forward, and it's all good. Personally, I had several tax years that were not filed. I contacted them, explained I was in custody, as well as my family's economic situation. My family was doing their best to stay afloat, while the family breadwinner was in custody. I filed all my old returns when I got out. They gave me a reasonable payment plan. End of story. We move on.

Reason #6 - "All Debt Instruments Are Not The Same"

There's a big misunderstanding between the use of debt versus the wise use of leverage. There's a reason for using debt instruments like credit cards as well as financing automobiles and homes, but they are not all the same. It is true that upon concluding a transaction with anyone of them, you will end up owing money to someone. You will have various options and methods to pay, but that's about all they have in common. This misunderstanding and misuse of credit card debt have resulted in Americans carrying enormous amounts of revolving debt. This, in turn, compounds the problem by lowering credit scores and increasing interest rates—with you potentially becoming a slave to credit cards and other financial institution payments. The list goes on and on.

Don't get me wrong. Credit cards are an important tool, providing a very convenient way to purchase things. They can also provide you with your first red flag that something is not right with your finances. The point is, if you're not paying off your credit cards in full at the end of every month, you are *living beyond your means*. In other words, there is more money going out than coming into your financial life. (see the article on page 281 about what this does to you)

A positive cash flow is essential to financial success and should always be the priority maintained. Credit cards are not instantaneous loans. They do have value with certain rebates, online convenience purchases, and the blessing of not having to carry cash. They also offer a way for huge companies to make lots of money off of the money you work hard for. If you are not strong-minded and stubborn, credit cards can and will set you up for total failure. The first step is to see that a credit card is not the same as a home mortgage or auto loan. Blowing your budget is the biggest disadvantage of credit cards in that they encourage people to spend money that they don't have. Credit card companies charge enormous amounts of interest on each balance that you don't pay off each month. On the other hand, certain debt, like home loan debt, has lots of advantages. Here's an example of what I call "The Wise Use of Leverage."

So Let's Buy A Home!

For most mortals like us, when you buy a home, you are not using your own money. You are using other people's money—money from the bank. This allows you to put down a small amount, the downpayment as it's called, and the bank will finance the rest. Home loans typically have long-term payment arrangements. *Amortization Schedules* is the fancy term for the chart that shows those arrangements. You can pay a very small amount each month and still have ownership of a fairly expensive asset. It's a good deal because homes (if you maintain them) typically appreciate over time. And bonus, the government gives you incentives by allowing you to deduct a portion of your mortgage interest from your taxes. That's why I call financing a home a wise use of leverage. Purchasing a home can be within your reach with proper planning, and most mortgage companies are not doing background checks. Let's look at this example:

Two people are each going to purchase a home. Both homes are the same size— same extras, same lot size, garages basically the same. Everything is the same, including the price of $100,000. Mr. & Mrs. Cashman are Buyer A, and Mr. & Mrs. Leverage are Buyer B. By the way, there are plenty of homes in the United States at a price tag of $100,000.

The Cashmans bought a home valued at $100,000 using all cash, which includes closing costs. The Cashmans were happy campers. They lived and enjoyed their home for ten years, and then they decided to sell it. The Cashmans were able to sell it for $200,000! Sweet! The transactions are as follows:

- Investment $100,000
- Sold for $200,000
- Profit or gain of $100,000 or 100% return without consideration of taxes and expenses

Mr. & Mrs. Leverage, on the other hand, purchased a similar home valued at $100,000 but choose to keep

$80,000 for investment. They used only $20,000 as a deposit on the house. They took out a mortgage for $80,000. Their monthly payment was $454.23, not including taxes and insurance. Mr. and Mrs. Leverage sold their home ten years later for $200,000. They had a balance of $66,033.05 still owed to the bank. After paying off the first mortgage, the net proceeds were $133,967 minus Mr. Leverage's $20,000. The transactions are as follows:

- Investment $20,000 of their money and $80,000 from the bank
- Sold for $200,000
- Monthly payments for 10 years: $54,507.60
- Paid back the bank $66,033.05
- Profit or gain of $59,459.35 without consideration of taxes, expenses or tax benefits

So, after all is said and done, the Cashmans doubled their money; on the other hand, the Leverage family made almost three times their money by using the bank's money. Plus, the Leverages invested the $80,000 in the S&P 500 for the entire 10 years, which returned 10% annually. This caused the Leverages' stock portfolio to rise to $216,563.32.

The Bottom Line - 10 Year Return

CASHMAN		LEVERAGE
$100,000	vs	**$196,024.72**

There's a big difference between credit card debt, installment notes (auto loans), and home mortgages (the wise use of leverage). Bottom Line: Misuse of credit cards destroys wealth. Automobiles are a depreciating asset and, in general, a very poor investment and not the best place to use the bank's money. When it comes to automobiles, the best thing to do is buy high quality used cars, if you can, with all cash. Appreciating assets or assets that can generate income are the best for financing. Just remember, "Just because they all have an amount owed and monthly payments.....All debt is not the same."

Reason #7 - Failure to Manage and Understand Risk

Generally, everyone has some understanding of the meaning of the word 'risk.' As children, we are taught that something is risky, or we are told not to take risks. But what exactly is 'a risk'? We all do things knowing that there is a risk. We go to sleep at night, and somehow we are able to deal with the risk of not knowing if we will wake up the following morning. Ask anyone who's been in custody— you know that to be a fact. Fortunately for me, no one was killed while in reception, although many were severely beaten. In Jamestown, I never witnessed any deaths. But a riot broke out just before I arrived and someone lost his life. Upon my return to Jamestown, after serving 28 months in fire camp, a young man of 19 lost his life over a gambling debt. The word on the yard was a DP (a prison term for inmates issued a disciplinary action) gone bad. The bottom line: being in custody is not a safe experience. But before I get too far off course here, managing risk is a key component to rebuilding your wealth. If you don't manage your risks, you can start accumulating wealth, feeling good that things are going well. And BAM! Some surprise comes along and wipes out your bank account. Maybe it was an unknown like child support, the IRS, a car accident, or illness.

There are many methods for managing risk. Risk management is a very complicated subject. There are literally thousands of books on the subject. But for this book and your recovery, we will keep it short and sweet and to the point. On the other hand, that doesn't mean you should quickly read this section. This is a section to read slowly and consider each of these methods for dealing with risk.

There are four basic methods to deal with risk. First, you have to realize that there is a risk. Sometimes ignorance is bliss, but once you have identified the risk (child support, IRS, being physically attacked), you have basically 4 strategies.

You can *accept* the risk, eg. You decide to go surfing in shark-infested waters. There's a risk of a shark attack. Other risks include a surfboard accident with another surfer, a wave crushing you, or accidentally drowning. But people surf in conditions like this all the time and accept the risks all the time.

The second method is just to *avoid* the risk, eg. Just don't do it. Just do not go surfing. Of course, if you're in custody, you may not have that luxury anyhow.

The third method is to *reduce* the risk, eg. If we talk about driving a car, you would want to reduce the risk of getting hurt in an accident by wearing a seat belt. If you are surfing, you can practice safe surfing skills, go with a buddy and watch each other's back, and only surf on days where the waves or currents are calmer. In custody, every day is a risk. But you can reduce your exposure by doing your best to stay on your own, without the need to ask anyone for anything. Try not to get caught up in the politics and wherever possible roll with the Christian groups. In custody, this is a day to day challenge, but I can share from my own experience that you should stay away from anything to do with gambling and drugs (including tobacco). Keep an inventory of Ramen Soup for needed transactions and donations, and make sure you have a shadow when talking to an officer.

The fourth method is the *transfer* the risk to a third party using the wise use of insurance, eg. If you are concerned about the financial loss if you get eaten by a shark or accidentally drown, you can buy a life insurance policy or accidental death policy, which would create wealth for your family in the event of your death. By the way, there are companies that will insure inmates, but the policies are very expensive. If you know you're going to prison and shit can happen, it may be worth it— especially if you are out on bail awaiting trial. You must carefully analyze the cost-benefit. The other thing to note and we will get into this in detail a little bit later on in the book is that you only want to insure things that you cannot afford to lose. Just note that thought, and we will be getting back to that later in our discussion of "The E Fund."

I think you have to say to yourself that there's a risk in almost everything we do. You walk to the store; there's a risk you can fall and hurt yourself. You spend good money on some expensive electronic device; there's a risk that it will break or get lost or stolen. There's a risk when you commit a crime. There's a risk when you buy an investment. What do we do? What do we insure? Do we accept all the risks? Every person has a different risk tolerance. Financially, the general rule of thumb is that you want to avoid risk, use a risk-reduction strategy to reduce the risk, or insure the things you cannot afford to lose. Things you cannot afford to lose are things that, if they go wrong, will blow your financial plans.

REASON #8 - INFLATION:
   THE SILENT KILLER OF FINANCIAL PLANNING

Do you remember the 5¢ hamburger and a 40¢/hour minimum wage? How about a quarter for a gallon of gasoline? Probably not. But I've seen a tremendous amount of inflation in my lifetime. Did it ruin the investment climate? I think not. But the prices you see above are real numbers. So if you're not keeping up with inflation, you can end up working really hard and still be going backward.

You can't see it, but it's there. Over time inflation can be a huge unseen risk to your lifestyle and other areas of your finances. Going back all the way to 1871, according to data from Robert Shiller, inflation has averaged 2.1% per year. Since 1945, it's been higher than that coming in at around 3.9% a year. Inflation is simply a general rise in prices. It means that over time, your current money will buy fewer goods and services in the future. Inflation is one of the main reasons you need to save and invest for the future.

On the other hand, if you just put all the money you earned under your mattress and stopped working, it would slowly lose value over time. It's also the reason that cash should be looked at as an asset but not an investment. Inflation is why so many retired people over time have to lower their standard of living. They did not keep pace with inflation. In the course of your recovery, you will need to keep pace with inflation. But for most of you, I have calculated *36 critical months* to turn around your life. Inflation needs to be dealt with, but, for now, it's beyond the scope of this book.

Reason #9 - Procrastination:
The Cost of Procrastination

Tip: Don't put it off. "Putting off an easy thing makes it hard. Putting off a hard thing makes it impossible." -George Claude Lorimer

Some of us share a common experience. You're driving along when a police cruiser pulls up behind you with its lights flashing. You pull over, the officer gets out, and your heart drops: You're not just anyone being pulled over; you're a felon being pulled over. "Are you aware the registration on your car has expired?" You've experienced one of the costs of procrastination. Procrastination can cause a flash incarceration, a substantial fine, a trip to the court, a long line at the DMV, missed deadlines, missed opportunities, and just plain missing out.

Procrastination is avoiding important tasks. Important tasks need to be taken care of. You want to take care of them before they become emergencies, when you have no choice but to do them now! Procrastinators can sabotage themselves. They often put obstacles in their own path. They may choose paths that hurt their performance. Now or later. Mark Twain famously quipped, "Never put off until tomorrow what you can do the day after tomorrow." We know that procrastination can be detrimental, both in our personal and professional lives. Problems with procrastination in the business world have led to a sizable industry in books, articles, workshops, videos, and other products created to deal with the issue. There are many theories about why people procrastinate. Whatever the psychology behind it, procrastination has a big-time cost— personally, financially, with friends, with family, and spiritually.

> Everything in the world, whatever is and whatever happens, is a test, designed to give you freedom of choice. You Need to Choose Wisely.
>
> Rebbe Nachman of Breslov

*Putting important things off is **NOT** a very wise choice at all.*

CHAPTER 3

Establishing Goals and Objectives

God, grant me the serenity to accept the things I cannot change, Courage to change the things I can, and the Wisdom to know the difference.

Basically, there are three stages in the financial part of your life. The first stage is "the *learning* years." This covers the time from your birth to the financial separation from your parents, who provided everything for you. With few exceptions, most of us during the learning years were provided with food, clothing, the roof over your head, transportation, education, etc.

The second stage of your financial life is called "the *earning* years." The earning years are the years when all the responsibility is transferred to you. You are now responsible and expected to feed yourself, to buy your own clothing, provide for your own transportation, shelter, and so on. This a very important time in your financial life. The way you manage your *earning* years has a direct reflection on the third stage of your life. The third stage can either be called the *golden* years or the *yearning* years, depending on how you managed your time and efforts.

Powered with that thought, you can see that a critical component to getting the most out of life is setting goals and objectives during the later *learning* years and early *earning* years (**and** knowing the process of how to accomplish those goals). That is what this book is really all about. If you want to change your life, it's critically important to master the skills needed to get the things done that are a priority—personally, financially, and spiritually.

Unfortunately, our judicial system seems to take this approach: Since you have made a serious mistake or committed a crime, it is best to remove you from the earning years and push you back down to the learning years. I wonder if that was where the term "how long have you been down" originated. The government now becomes your parent who provides food, shelter, clothing, and no safety. But this time there is a big difference, unlike most parents whose best wishes are for your success and independence, the government guardians don't really care. They do very little in the way of protecting you while you're in custody and do very little (or no) preparation to help you become an independent self-sustaining, self-respecting member of society. Here's what really happens:

- you are placed in a racist political system to stay safe;
- your reputation now has a huge scar;
- there's no trade or employment placement system; and
- you have a very poor health care system.

The rehabilitation programs that they spend lots of money on sound good, but they are just nicely printed brochures. In reality, the programs are nothing but simple eyewash with no leadership or real desire to help. The worst part of all is that the environment is just not safe. In fact, in nearly all cases, upon your release, you're left in worse shape physically and mentally than when the whole process began. Sometimes I don't even see how it can be called the Department of Corrections. It's more like the Department of Destruction. The California system is a revolving door, and the problem starts at the top. So my advice to you is to stay safe, socialize to a minimum, and take advantage of the time in custody to prepare yourself. Get ready and be ahead of the pack. Start thinking now about what you want to do. Start thinking about how much you need to earn. Think about your family and friends. Do some soul searching.

And most importantly, consider your spiritual growth. No matter how far you have strayed, you can always return to God. I know that sometimes the situation you are in makes you question your beliefs. He's still there. All you need to do is reach out and talk. Talk privately or with a group, but talk to Him. Share your feelings, share your desires with all your heart, and pray, because God is always there.

Balancing The Four Corners

Although this book is titled *A Felon's Guide to Financial Recovery*, it's not all about the money. I call it "balancing the four corners of your life." You may ask me "why," and I'm glad you did. Just considering financial goals isn't enough or realistic. People need money, that's true. But they also need a quality network of friends and family. Everyone needs to stay healthy. I mean, what good is all of this work if you don't take care of yourself? And you need to have faith. I can't emphasize this enough: we are not in control. Therefore you need to worship and pray to the One who is.

If you look at the blank chart on page 59, you will see four quadrants. One labeled **Personal** is for personal goals. Another marked **Business** is for business-related goals. **Family and Friends** and **Spiritual** are the last two areas. We will be making a list of what you want to accomplish in each area. We will consider a short and medium period of time, being very careful not to plan beyond three or four years. Planning too far ahead is just not practical when exiting custody. Lots of things change and change pretty quickly from my personal experience.

But before we do all of this, I'd like you to think about people you know who put all their energy into just one of the quadrants. For example, a person who doesn't care about anyone else may not care about how they earn their money. As long as they get what they want personally — even at the expense of others— the rest doesn't matter. They may have no belief in God. They think they are in control of everything. Let's forget friends and family; they are a total distraction and burden. It doesn't sound like someone I'd want to hang with. Or how about the person who put all their energy into thinking about money 24/7? They literally worship the all mighty dollar while they neglect their personal health, their family, friends, and God. Or what about the person who spends all their time caring for others and forgets to take care of themselves? In the end, they become a charity case themselves— mentally, physically, financially, and emotionally. They can't even function as caregivers anymore. And lastly, what about the person so engrossed in their church or religious beliefs that they neglect themselves and everything else.

My experience has shown that to be successful and have that deep-rooted happiness—the happiness you can feel internally—you need to have balance in the four corners of your life. You need to set *personal* goals, *business* goals, *spiritual* goals and goals for *family and friends*. It has been my experience as a professional financial planner, that those who balance the four corners have a success rate ten fold over those who consider only money and money-related items.

It's time to get out that piece of paper! Keep it in your pocket with your pencil and pen. You can keep it on your rack, or if you're lucky, maybe you have a locker. Keep it safe. Remember how many times something happens in the dorm, and all your stuff is thrown everywhere? This is an important list—maybe you should just keep it in your pocket, or in your sock if no pockets are available. Maybe put it in a plastic lunch bag. Just keep it safe and personal.

Personal	Business

| Family & Friends | Spiritual |

Setting Personal Goals and Objectives

Now let's start setting some personal goals. Starting thinking about what you want to do for yourself personally. Think about what you want to achieve in your life. Separating what's important to you from what's not, get out your paper and pen, and start thinking and writing. Write down your goals because you're going to find out that setting goals is only one part of the process. It's the most important part! If you don't know where you're going, you might as well just drive anywhere. The second part of the process, achieving the goal, puts you in your "happy place." Once the goal is completed, you are motivated to do more. This causes your self-confidence to go way up, and you want to achieve even more. Want to change your life? It starts right here, right now. When you set personal goals to improve your life, you gain direction in life. Goals give meaning to every day, and reflecting on even the smallest of successes can create great pleasure. It can turn a bad day into a great day! *Even in custody*, goal setting gives your life a purpose and develops so much positive energy. It can turbocharge your attitude and avoid "Bad Days and Hard Time."

Everyone has their own list of things they want to achieve, but here are a few examples to consider. Think about what you want to plan to get done from the next 3 months to the next 3 years.

Examples of Personal Goals:
- ☐ Get yourself into an exercise routine that's not based upon mandatory requirements
- ☐ Try to eat healthier
- ☐ Find a place to live or a new home
- ☐ Improve your current living situation
- ☐ Find transportation
- ☐ Learn how to meditate
- ☐ Learn how to get a better night's sleep
- ☐ Learn how to get more things done in a day
- ☐ Learn how to get rid of toxic people surrounding you without getting beat up
- ☐ Learn a new skill
- ☐ Learn a new language or trade
- ☐ Find a new girlfriend or boyfriend

Everyone's list will be different. Take a moment and write some of those things down right now for the next 3 months to the next 3 years. If you can't think of anything right now, no worries, just keep the paper and pen in your pocket or nearby when you go to bed and when the idea comes into your head, write it down. I keep a pad and pen near my bed every day because sometimes I wake up in the middle of the night with a great idea and start stressing about forgetting it. I just get up, write it out, and then a few minutes later go back to sleep. If I don't do that, I can be up for the rest of the night— with my head going a mile a minute.

Business Goals and Objectives

The title of this book is *A Felon's Guide to Financial Recovery*, and no doubt, we have a high emphasis on money. But this area must be realistic when you are financially starting over or walking through the gates of freedom. Although all of you have different circumstances, this is a recovery book for those who are starting over from scratch. And although we would all like to sing the song "I want to be a billionaire, so freakin bad," it is just not reality. So in this section, we are going to remain extremely sober. Rather than write down that you want to be a billionaire, I am going to suggest a set of guidelines. We will start with your prospective income (money yet to be made) by answering the question: **How much money do I need?**

Let's Pause for a second and think about that ...This is a very important number. It needs to be realistic and legitimate. How you earn it may have to be approved by probation/parole. So rather than just picking a number, I developed a system that works. It's worked for me personally as well as other inmates. We get the right number by working backward and estimating your expenses. We are going to call this process the X treatment— "X" being how much money you will need at specific times. We are going to figure out the amounts in advance, look at a bunch of numbers, do some easy calculations, and fill in the magic numbers.

But in the meantime, I think it's very important for you to put something in the business goals quadrant now. You make the call. You can list what you wish. It can always be changed later, or you can use my highly recommended method. If you decided to use my method, go to your goals chart and *write the following in Quadrant II*: I need a job or a business that will generate X for the first six months, X for the next six to eighteen months and X for eighteen months and beyond. We will come back and fill in the X's later. The time is broken down into specific periods. They are all important periods of time, but no doubt, the most critical period is the first 6 months. We have a separate financial goal to meet just for the first 6 months.

By the way, some of you might achieve this in the first month, for others it may take a year. This is just a block of time. It would be totally fantastic if you were able to pull the financial trigger on your first 6 months, prepared and ready to go, **while you were still in custody!** "Huge." It takes a lot of work, but it can be done.

So, if you haven't written it yet: I need a job or a business that will generate X for the first six months, X for the next six to eighteen months and X for eighteen months and beyond.

Family and Friends

For most of us, being in custody challenged our valued relationships with our families and friends. Let's be straight up on this: we lied, we cheated, some of us have stolen. We may have acted inappropriately psychologically and physically with our mothers, fathers, sisters, brothers, wives, husbands, and significant others. It's time for forgiveness, patience, honesty, and love—so many of the needed character traits to repair the trust that has been broken. You may have made promises to your children that weren't kept. You may have a strained relationship that you believe is beyond repair. You may be right, but these are your parents, friends, relatives, siblings, spouse, or significant others.

You need to throw that kind of thinking out the window and start to reevaluate each and every one of these priceless relationships. Get out a piece of paper and start writing down names and next to each maybe how you think you let them down. Get on the phone, and start asking family members to put some money on the phone. If that's not available, start writing letters and begin the mending process now. Remember, phone calls to prison are expensive. You want to plan the conversations in advance and get the most out of your calls. This can take days, months, even years, but the last thing you want to do is wait for your release to start figuring this out. Make a list of all your family and friends that you consider to have a relationship with. Next, write down what you think the relationship is with that person. Next to that, write down what you did to cause the issue: lie, cheat, steal, etc. Then add what you would want to accomplish with each of them. If you value the relationship, it requires energy to fix this. The best way to do that is to be organized, honest, and upfront.

Examples: Reach out and write or call your parents. Get involved with your children. Make peace with the family (mother, father, grandparents, and siblings) or your baby's momma's family. Ask them to put money on the phone for you or for commissary or canteen. Take small steps and be thankful for every step of the way.

As we continue on with this book, you will find out that family and friends are a major asset. When you're released, you are going to need help. Don't expect the County, Federal, or State Governments to help. Start repairing and building stronger relationships right now! Get out your paper and write down the things you want to accomplish with family and friends.

Spiritual (The Anchor)

As a twenty-five year professional financial planner, I say to you now, that without doubt you need faith in your life or you will not be successful. I've seen people become millionaires and billionaires and then saw those same people succeeding or falling off the deep end. Those that stayed grounded have become the pillars of their families and communities, and those successes all have one thing in common "strong faith." Those that do not are governed by animal instincts and fall into the trap of an abusive mentality. There's a reason for everything, even being in custody. Although thinking about yourself is important, it's not really all about you and me. It's about you and your place in the community and God's purpose for your life. You will not find those answers from our employers, the government, or anyone else. The answers come to your own soul from the Lord, our God. Let faith be your anchor. When your world is fractured, it's time to increase your knowledge of God. It will bring you inner peace and greater strength during this transitionary time. Spiritual goals are not just attending religious services; it's about becoming a better person. You want the transformation of your soul to become more honest, patient, humble, kind, generous, and not to be lazy—just to name a few. Faith will be your anchor, your strength, your guiding light to hope.

Any architect knows that a solid foundation is essential to any building. In Luke 6, Jesus explains the difference between a wise builder and a foolish one. A builder who is wise hears the Word of God, applies it to their own life, and as a result, stands firmly through turbulent times. However, the foolish builder doesn't obey or apply God's principles and instructions. He's ruined when a raging storm hits his life. Your spiritual foundation is vital to your life and following God and submitting to His wisdom enables you to build a solid foundation based on His values. As you base your life on Him, there are few areas you need to focus on to cultivate a strong, healthy spiritual life. This won't only benefit you; others will reap the blessings as well.

Your relationship with God will have a profound effect on personal and financial goals. Here are a few things to consider.

Your Faith: Your trust in God, your growing relationship with Him, and your obedience to and application of God's Word are all crucial to building a solid foundation of faith. When the storms of life come your way, you will be grounded in biblical truths and remain steady as a rock on your moral beliefs. Plus, you will stay strong inwardly by trusting in God's sovereignty. If you disobey Him, your foundation will begin to crack. For this reason, it's always wise to seek God daily.

Your Health: Your body is God's living temple; His Spirit resides within you. When you harm your body, you're dishonoring God. Keeping your body healthy is a spiritual discipline that is part of the life God calls you to. Living a healthy lifestyle also permits you to carry out God's greater plans for your life.

Finances: Being a good steward over your finances is a spiritual discipline that blesses God, others, and you. Living outside of your means, amassing material possessions, and accumulating irresponsible debt are unwise. When you manage your finances wisely, *you eliminate needless stress.*

Family and Friends: Relationships are vital and should be cherished! The people in your life — and your relationship with them — are important to God. They need to be valued and esteemed fittingly. God desires that you love others and seek to build them up, not tear them down. And knowing that "bad company corrupts good character," be careful who you spend time with.

> Are you faithful? Ask yourself this question: If I was put on trial from my religious beliefs, would there be enough evidence to convict me?

I have a few inspiring quotes to help you with your spiritual journey.

- Spiritual awakening begins with inspiration coming from without. Then, once you are already on the road, the real work begins. Keep at it, and inspiration will then come from within.
- In the early stages of your spiritual journey, it may seem that Heaven is rejecting you and spurning all your efforts. Stay on course. Don't give up. In time, all barriers will disappear.

- Growing spiritually can be like a roller coaster ride. Take comfort in the knowledge that the way down is on preparation for the way up.
- Go Carefully: Spiritual growth must proceed slowly and steadily. Too often, we want to improve ourselves and our relationships so quickly that we make ourselves frustrated and confused.
- Never insist that everything go exactly your way, even in spiritual matters.
- Believe that none of the effort you put into coming closer to God is ever wasted—even if, in the end, you don't achieve what you are striving for.
- Always remember: You are never given an obstacle you cannot overcome.
- Occupy yourself with doing good, and the bad will automatically fall away.

Now take a few minutes to write down your spiritual goals— what you would like to accomplish over the next 3 months and over the next 3 years.

Make yourself a chart to give yourself a visual. I have included blank pages in the back of the book because I know how hard it is sometimes to get writing paper in custody. But before you go and write in the book, if you can get some writing paper instead, take out a piece of paper. Then either use a pen or your golfer pencil. I prefer the golfer pencil along with an eraser because you will be erasing, making changes, and additions. Title the page **Goals and Objectives 3 months thru 3 years**. Then underneath the title, draw a cross and start listing your goals and objectives for the next 3 months until the next 36 months, using the four categories listed below.

- Top Left: Personal Goals - Quadrant I
- Top Right: Business Goals - Quadrant II
- Bottom Left: Family and Friends Goals - Quadrant III
- Bottom Right: Spiritual Goals - Quadrant IV

Write down what you want to accomplish in the short term (first 3 months) and then below that list the goals, up to and including the next 36 months. If your release date is beyond the next 6 months, the good news is that you have more time to get your ducks in order. No matter what your term is, even if you are being released tomorrow, you have work to do. So start listing what you want to change, learn, and do. This is the first step. And it's the most important step. As we said in the beginning, without a destination, you're just getting in a car every day and driving nowhere.

Don't be tough on yourself here, be creative, loose, and light-minded. You have an eraser? If not, order one from the canteen. Or look for someone who is being released. Sometimes they just leave them around. Or you can try to borrow one. Defining your goals at this point should not be considered a permanent life change. Life is not a ratchet wrench.

It ebbs and flows. So while you're in the process of defining your goals (in the goal mode, so to speak), remember that tomorrow you're probably going to wake up with new ideas. Be prepared to make plenty of changes. Believe it or not, that's a good thing because you're considering new priorities, and this is all part of the process. Eventually, after the dust settles (and it can take a few days or a few weeks), you will have a pretty good list in each of the four quadrants. Get out your eraser or just add something new to the list. There are no wrong answers here because it's all you.

This is a great time to take a break!

Time To Prioritize

Once you have created your lists, you are ready to move on to the next two steps in the process: Categorizing and Prioritizing. This is a very important part of the process involved in defining the goals and creating the lists because it forces you to decide what items are the most important to deal with first. Without the categories and priorities, we just have a list. Remember when we talked about the roadmap for the trip to San Francisco? We said that you would need to secure your method of transportation before getting started on the journey. A trip by automobile is a whole different trip than going by boat or plane.

Let's start by first breaking down each of your goals listed in each of the four quadrants. Each goal should fall into one of three different categories: A, B, or C:

- ☐ A = Emergencies
  (Things you must do right now!)
- ☐ B = Important
  (Things you should be doing now.)
- ☐ C = Like to do
  (Things you would like to do when you have the time.)

This should be done for each goal in each of the four quadrants independently.

That's a mouthful, so let's try and make some sense out of it. The best way to learn this part of the process is for you to go to your list and identify what goals you think are emergencies, what goals you think are important, and what goals are things you would like to do. Take a moment and mark each one of your goals as an A, B, or C. It's a great exercise. Remember, you are doing this within each quadrant —independent of the others. At the end of this step, you will have four separate lists of categorized and prioritized goals: one for personal goals, one for business goals, one for family goals, and one for spiritual goals. Now that you have categorized and prioritized your goals, it's time for a practical explanation. Be prepared to have your eraser handy!

Is it really an emergency? Many of the people you know live in what I call the "world of emergency." They think everything is an emergency. Let me define what an emergency is or what it *should be* for our purposes. An emergency is something that, if you do not do it at this very moment, you're going to have a very serious repercussion (your screwed). For example, you're living in an all-wood home, and suddenly a trash can near the wall catches fire. If you do not put that fire out right now, you're screwed. *That's an emergency.* That's a category A. Think of the Emergency Room. Many people visit the emergency room and are willing to sit for hours, just because they are not feeling well that day. They want to see a doctor. But that's not an emergency—that's a regular doctor's visit. On the other hand, if you have someone going into cardiac arrest, and if they don't get to the emergency room quickly, they are going to die. That's an emergency.

But as I mentioned above, we all know people who live in a world of emergency all the time. They think everything is an emergency. I call it the living in the land of "A's" because they never get anything done. They are always chasing some emergency or what they think is an emergency. They wait to the last minute to leave for a party. They are always under stress driving because they worry that they will be late. This type of mentality is not only unhealthy but habit-forming. If you are one of the majority in custody with substance issues, you know the feeling of your heart pumping a mile a minute chasing the next emergency. You do not want to live in that world. That's the world of addiction.

You do want to live in the world of doing what's **important**. This is a fundamental concept because it prepares you mentally to start thinking proactively, not reactively. Important things are important things to do. **I call it the Land of the "B's."** These are things you *should* be doing, like planning to go out, planning to leave by a certain time to get somewhere on time. Some things may take a few days, weeks, or months to get done. But I can tell you this, there's a lot of long-lasting internal happiness in planning and accomplishing your goals proactively. And it is the complete opposite of living in the world of emergency.

Every successful business person lives in the Land of the "B." They do what is important every day. They do most things because they want to and not because they have to. The whole focus of planning is all about thinking, planning, *and then* doing "not just doing." If you do what is important every day, you avoid having emergencies.

A good example is changing tires. If you keep neglecting your tires, you will either end up with a fix-it ticket or a blow out in the middle of traffic. At that point, you need to stop regardless of what's going on in your life. It becomes an emergency. Your routine automobile maintenance is a B. But if you neglect it, it turns into an A. The other added bonus about Living in the world of B is you get a much better night's restful sleep. You're not worried about what you have to do. As life gets even better, your sleep gets better, which in turn keeps you healthier and more alert. When your health is on point with a good night's rest, you're more likely to make better decisions in general.

Lastly, the "C" category are the things you would like to do, but may not be feasible at this time. Wanting to buy a new car while it's just not within your financial ability is a "C." Or it could also be something like wanting to go out of town with your children on vacation, but you're on parole, and your parole officer has told you that you must stay in the county. Those things are fairly easy to mark as a "C." Now go back to your list and remark all your goals with the appropriate A, B, or C. Once you're done, come right back to this spot, we're not done yet.

Which One Comes First?

Now that you have *categorized* your goals, you need to *prioritize* your goals into what items should be dealt with first. They are all important, but realistically you may be starting from scratch and will not have the means to do all of these things the moment you cross over into the world of freedom. That doesn't mean they won't get done. It does mean that you need to have plenty of patience—something most inmates learn almost immediately while in custody.

So with that being said, be aware, you need to go forward carefully, you must proceed slowly and steadily. Too often, we want to improve ourselves and our relationships so quickly that we make ourselves frustrated and confused. In these conditions, you can never insist that everything go exactly your way. If you have to choose between patience and anxiety, always choose patience. So now, go back to your list and mark each goal in priority order. The chart below gives you an example of what it should look like.

Personal	*Business*
Eat healthiest possible diet B1	Business or Employment income of X per month for the first 6 months. B1
Exercise B2	
Start a business B3	
	Business or Employment income of X per month for 6 to 18 months. B2
	Business or Employment income of X per month for 18 months and beyond. B3
Family & Friends	**Spiritual**
Rebuild my relationship with my parents. B1	Work daily on my relationship with God. B1
Rebuild my relationship with my baby's momma's parents. B2	Participate in Bible Study. B2
Get Married. C1	Work on strengthening my soul traits e.g. Patience, Humility, Kindness, etc. B3
Take my children to Disneyland. C2	

To Recap:
- Identify your goals or objectives
- Classify those goals as either an
- A-Emergency,
- B- Something Important and or
- C-Something You Would Like To Do

Take each goal one at a time and place them into priority order in each quadrant.

Ok, Now Freeze!

There is one more big item to deal with before we can move on. **What's That? That's Right!** We need to discuss substance abuse. Did you list your issues with substance abuse as A1 top priority? If you did, my hat's off to you! You are a very rare breed indeed. That issue is a definite A. No it's not a fire burning in a wood home— it's worse. It's worse because you are not being honest with yourself. (It's like not even acknowledging that there is a fire in the house!) Think about it, you have just been asked to list all the goals you personally wanted to accomplish. You have placed them in priority order. How can that be the truth if your primary function every day is to find some way, somehow, to make yourself functional by figuring out how to obtain a substance? 80-90% of the prison population has issues with substance abuse.

My neighbor in Dorm 4 Jamestown just spent 2 plus years in prison, he was scheduled to get out a week before me. I asked him what he was going to do first when he got out. He said he was going to buy a pack of cigarettes! That was all he was thinking about. Plus, this guy was in prison because of multiple DUI's! Substance abuse is a bear. It is very, very tough to deal with. This book is not even going to attempt to try and fix those issues. But I can tell you this, the monkey will never be off your back. If you are addicted to anything, the hunger will never ever go away. What you need to do is learn to cope with it. I started smoking when I was 10 years old, and I was fully addicted by 14. Then I gave them up starting at the age of 25, and it took me 5 freakin years of aggravating hard work to learn how to cope and live without them. To this day, I can not smoke or chew or anything that has anything to do with tobacco. Being in custody is the perfect place and time to give up tobacco. It's a great start—unless you really enjoy having to smoke Pig Spit that you or someone scraped out of a trash can or off the floor, or tobacco that has been shoved up someone's asshole (anus, rectum, mud hole, the prison pocket, the hoop, etc.)... and using toilet tissue rolls or pages from the Bible to smoke it! ARE YOU KIDDING ME !!!. Once you are released, you will have a choice. You can march right down to the closest gas station and take 10% of that precious money you've just been given and buy a pack and put your addiction back into heavy hunger mode. Get past it, don't do it. The new vaping pens are just as bad. All of this has to go away.

Smoking, drugs. It all has to go! I'm 66 years old and haven't smoked in 36 years, and I know I STILL CAN'T HANDLE IT! Address your substance abuse issues first. Start building your will power now and don't buy the weirdo thing when you don't participate with your prison compadres. If you don't give this stuff up, you will be building a house on a deck of cards that will eventually fall. It's like every day walking on very thin ice—you're going to fail. It is just a question of when. Heroin, Cocaine, Fentanyl... Jimmy Hendrix, Robin Williams, Whitney Houston, Tom Petty, Michael Jackson, and the list goes on. You will be in an out of prison/custody for the rest of your life. Rise above it, use God's strength. Pass Him your burden, make Him your crutch, and learn to cope. I'm still an addict but have been clean for over 36 years. Time to grow up.

Now go back to your list and make the adjustment and let's move on. Don't get me wrong. To honor another is to see the Divine in that person, no matter what their circumstance or behavior. This, of course, doesn't mean we condone bad behavior; it does, however, mean we don't see others as 'less than.'

As a professional counselor, I work with people struggling with addiction. So often we blame people for their choices without considering the person in front of us– one who may be down and out on their luck or may have turned to drugs or alcohol to manage stress or trauma. I have come to know that no one plans to be a person with a substance use disorder. It takes tremendous courage and strength for people struggling with addiction to admit they need help and to be willing to do whatever it takes to battle this disease. What people struggling with addiction do not need is to be condemned. On the contrary, they need understanding and support; they need mutual respect and assistance; and they need to be honored for the souls that they are. There I have said my peace.

Now that we have established the most important part of the financial planning process (establishing your goals and objectives), the next step encompasses two of the six parts we discussed. We need to Clarify Your Present Situation and Identify Financial Problems. I call it Establishing Your Current Status.

CHAPTER 4

Establishing Your Current Status

With a focus on the financial, where are you financially right now? There are lots of ways to look at establishing your current financial situation. But we are doing our best to keep this process as simple as possible. My very first business, which I started in my early 20's was in the photo processing business. Believe it or not, people used to take pictures with cameras and film and then drop the film off at a photo shop, drug store, or candy store. My company, RDS Photo, would pick up the film, process it, and turn the rolls and cartridges of film into negatives and photographs. "Snap Shots"— that's what they were called. Snap a picture, and you had a frozen moment in time.

For those that remember when there was no video, no YouTube, no iPhone, you might remember 8mm movie film. Film is, of course, still available today sort of as a hobby. And movie film is still used for today's mainstream motion pictures, keeping a non-magnetic permanent record (though how long that will last is anyone's guess). But movies are not standing still like a snapshot they are moving.

I have a tendency to think of things in photographic terms. You may have heard the financial term **income and expenses** or **cash flow.** What I'm suggesting is that you think of *cash flow* as the **motion picture** of your financial life, because it is always moving. Just like a motion picture is always moving, so does your income and expenses. Every day, all day, your resources are coming in (income) or going out (expenses). The income is generated for most of us by jobs, business income, work, pensions, interest, or social service benefits. At the same time, resources are flowing out to pay bills, buy gas, etc. (expenses) and resources are constantly being used. Money In, Money Out.

The other term you need to focus on is your **net worth**, aka your **assets and liabilities.** Your *net worth* is like the **snapshot** of your financial life. Your freeze-frame snapshot is like halting time and counting your beans. How much cash do you have on hand at this particular moment? How much money do you owe? In the current status part of the process, we are interested in gathering the information that will establish (as best as we can) where you are right now.

The Motion Picture

Below, I have taken the liberty of establishing an income target for you. If you recall in the previous chapter, The "X" Method, what we are trying to do is work backward to fill in the "X's." To do that, we establish your business goals based upon your anticipated expenses, rather than the other way around. Most people think like this: "I make so much money, and this is how much I can spend with it." I am suggesting the reverse: "This is how much I need, now I need to figure out how to get it."

Think about it, if you don't plan your expenses first and realize how much you will need, how do you know if the job offered is the right fit for you? Or are you someone who doesn't care? You just take anything that comes your way because it's money, and you need it. "It's an emergency."

If you are planning to go into your own business, how will you know how much to charge and if the amount charged is enough? So start by planning your expenses in advance. It becomes the key to understanding your income needs, not the other way around.

We all come from different economic backgrounds and examples, typically set by our parents and their parents before them. Some of you may be shocked at the target expenses. Don't be, they are being used only as a guide. This is a real-life guide; it's there to help you realize what you're not paying for right now while you are in custody. That, in turn, should help you to be more mentally prepared for real life. Economically things will be very different upon your release. There's a lot to be learned here, so take your time and think about all this.

We are going to take it a step further so that we can go back and fill in the "X's". If you recall, we are going to establish your financial needs within three different time periods. These time periods will vary case by case, but, generally:

- ☐ Start Your Engine - The most critical time being your first 6 months of freedom,
- ☐ Try to Keep the Engine Going with Very Low Fuel and Battery - 6 months to 18 months, and finally
- ☐ Your Motor is Running - 18 months and beyond.

Let's take a closer look at the chart on the next page and see what it's costing you while you are in custody right now and how that actually compares to real life. Everyone will have there own set of numbers, but I have taken liberties here and plugged in numbers based upon 25 years in the financial services and counseling thousands of clients. As a professional financial planner, I was privileged and honored to review clients' confidential personal financial information. Understand that there is a basis for the numbers shown below. We are just going to assume your income is 0, starting from scratch. If you have one of the few available jobs at a conservation camp or you have additional income sources outside of custody, you are already ahead. But for most, they have lost their current job, and the promise to be rehired is just that, a promise. Getting a job and starting a business follow in the later chapters for now let's just focus on this Financial Motion Picture.

The Motion Picture of Income and Expenses

Monthly Income: $0

Monthly Expenses:

Expense	Earning Years	During Custody
Rent/Mortgage	$2000	$0
Food	$ 500	$0
Cellphone	$ 100	$0
Transportation	$ 300	$0
Fuel	$ 200	$0
Insurance	$ 100	$0
Personal Care	$ 20	$0
Laundry	$ 25	$0
Medical	$ 100	$0
Entertainment	$ 200	$0
Direct TV	$ 100	$0
Clothing	$ 200	$0
Home Expenses	$ 200	$0
Vacation	$ 100	$0
Gifts	$ 100	$0
Charity	$ 100	$0
Taxes	$?	$0

Saving and Investing – The Excess and Result of Good Work

So what we can gain and discuss from this pre-designed standard of living shown on the previous page? Let's start by looking at Rent/Mortgage of $2000 a month. This, for most of you, can be a shocking number. Does that mean that the plan is for you to be paying $2000 a month from the moment you are released? Absolutely not! What is does mean is that this is a target, a goal. And as we have discussed throughout this book, having goals is the key to success. As a side note, I'm not in favor of renting anything, but many people don't realize that they can own a home. In the course of my career, I've run across families who have been renting their entire lives and do it because they are just not comfortable with owning a house. Personally and professionally, I believe that homeownership is the key to long term rehabilitation and success. When you are a homeowner, you are an embedded, long-term part of your community, even if your neighbor is a police officer. Homeownership gives you a stake in, as they say, "there's skin in the deal." Keeping your neighborhood a clean and safe place to live becomes important to you. You are continually motivated to maintain the property because it's simple: failure to do so could reduce your property value. Homeownership becomes your own personal retirement investment. With all of that, you will have a much better chance of building a clean life and staying the course.

I will share several strategies that I have used personally and on behalf of clients on how to purchase a home for little or no money down (as of the date of this book— things can change). This will be useful if and when you earn enough money to pay a rent of $2000 per month. Remember, most of my clients were rich, but if they could get a piece of property without coming out of pocket, they jumped at it.

These numbers are all based upon California standards because that is where I have lived for the past 30 years. In general, California is pretty expensive. $2000 a month can get you a lot of house in Texas, Nevada, and other states. In the back section of the book, we have listed numerous states that potentially offer a much better standard of living compared to California.

While you are reading this, it's more important for you to realize that you are not living in the real world— you're living in an institution. Right now, you're paying zero for all your living expenses. There's no free lunch; it's simply not real. Don't get used to it! Some of you right now have just said to yourselves, "How can anyone get used to this?" But reality steps in and some do. In fact, while on the subject of social programs, prisons and jails are just another big social program. Don't get used to any of this. Many of my fellow inmates were willing to settle for a prison standard of living! "It's like the army," they told me. "You don't have to worry about food, clothing, or shelter." THIS IS NOT THE ARMY! Inmates start becoming institutionalized and start to lose their confidence, being beaten down all the time. NEVER GIVE UP! Start building your confidence and build up the energy needed to step up and earn a living near or equal to the one I have just prepared for you. Prison standards are just not reality. God has a purpose for your life. Your income won't be given to you on a silver platter. You will need to work smart. At times, you will need to work very hard. It doesn't happen overnight, and you probably won't get exactly what you want. The reward for earning and maintaining your own home and making an honest living is godly and priceless. Yes, if you go down the list above, you can always say I can live for way less. I agree, and you will most likely have to do just that, especially during the first 6 months. But you need set goals, and right now, these are pretty good benchmarks.

Let's briefly go through each of the other expenses just so that you get a good idea of how professional financial planners look at each individual expense.

Food and Groceries: $500/month. Again this is purposefully high, but it does include going out to fast-food restaurants as well as health and beauty aids and over the counter items like Ibuprofen. So when you start adding those items, that $500 number becomes a pretty good number.

- **Cellphone**: $100/month. This is also a little high, but very realistic. Consider the phone purchase as part of the service agreement. Plus, I am very big on Cell Phones. We will get into that a little later on.
- **Transportation, Fuel, and Insurance** really can be grouped together, $300, $200, and $100 /month, respectively. $300 for a New Car Loan, $200 for Gas and Oil Changes for the vehicle, and $100 for the right automobile insurance policy.
- **Personal Care**: $20/month. This is for a haircut, but realize most people don't get their haircut every month. So you're putting $20 aside for personal care whether you spend it or not. You've got money left over to do your nails or get a back massage.
- **Laundry**: $25/month. This is for washing your clothing and dry cleaning.
- **Medical**: $100/month. This is for a high deductible Heath Maintenance Organization, just to cover things you are unable to afford in the event something serious happens. This is a low amount, but we will go into it a bit more in detail later.
- **Entertainment**: $200/month. This is slotted to pay for streaming movie services, going out on a date, out to dinner, concerts, sporting events, etc.
- **Direct TV/Internet**: $100/month. Now this would be for a home internet or home TV service.
- **Clothing**: $200/month. Again, whether you spend it or not, this is to rebuild your wardrobe. It also includes things like watches, hats, and sunglasses.

Home: $200/month. This is for rebuilding the things you need at home: bed, TV, toaster, or other appliances. It's also for home upkeep expenses and repairs.

Vacation: $100/month. Yes, this is for a very modest vacation, something to recharge the batteries after working really hard.

Gifts: $100/month. This is one of the most overlooked expenses when planning a budget. Tell me who doesn't buy the Christmas Gift or Birthday Present? People do and many times are not financially prepared.

Charity: $100/month. It's important to give back. You have been blessed. This is simply a way to show you're thankful. How you choose to donate is entirely up to you.

Taxes are an unknown, just realize that if you are making money, you will be paying taxes. Personally, I don't like taxes, I don't like paying taxes, and I don't like preparing taxes. But taxes are important and must be planned for before they turn into emergencies.

Whatever is left over after that should be slotted for savings and investment. But in reality, it will be just for savings. It will become clearer as we move on.

Therefore, by the 36th month, your income target, based upon the expenses listed above, either through employment or residual business income, should be equal to or greater than $4345/month after taxes. Later on in the book, we will break it down even further. You should now go to Quadrant II and replace the X in the spot for 36 months and beyond with $4345.

IT'S TIME FOR FREEZE FRAME!

What is your Net Worth, BAM! Right at this moment? The financial snapshot of your assets and liabilities:

Assets
Cash on hand (CDCR Trust Funds)
Personal Property
Cash Value Life Insurance
Real Estate
Retirement Funds (IRA, 401K, 403b)
Stocks, Bonds, and Mutual Funds
Gold, Silver, and Jewelry
Business Ownerships

Liabilities
Taxes Due
Personal Loans (payable to people)
Corporate Loans (payable to companies)
Credit Cards
Child Support
Judgements Outstanding

The list on page 91 gives you a general idea of assets (useful or valuable things) and liabilities (things for which someone is responsible, especially a debt or financial obligation). The list does not breakdown in detail the individual assets or liabilities. For example, an automobile would be considered personal property. We didn't go into detail for two reasons. First of all, everyone has their own unique list— especially when it comes to personal property. Secondly, the reality is for most of us, we will be starting at ground zero. But it's helpful to detail as much as you can. At the end of this exercise, you should have assigned a value to each item on the list. This should give you a realistic snapshot of your assets and liabilities. By the way, if you subtract your liabilities from your assets, the answer results in your *Net Worth*.

If you're like most inmates, you're probably feeling quite depressed at this point since there's not much in the way of assets. You may even have a negative net worth due to restitution. And, on top of that, you're still going to need money to get back on your feet. So, unless you were lucky to get a job at fire camp, there may not be much in the way of assets coming your way while in custody. If you have a prison job, the good news is that you will have something to do. The bad news is that what you're being paid in prison isn't even enough to cover the things you need at the canteen or a decent package.

There is a brighter side. I have some really good news for a change. This will be worth the price and time you're putting into this book. We are going to discuss strategies to protect your assets so that you can level the playing field from known and unknown third parties. And, there may be other assets you may not have considered. So, pay close attention.

Other assets you may have not considered:
1. **Friends, Family, Business Associations, and Trade Experience: Do not underestimate the value of your relationships. These are Very, Very, Very Important Assets.** If you're at the beginning of this process, upon arrest, friends and family can join together to create a legal defense fund. In many cases, it can be large enough to provide for an entire legal defense team. Your family and friends can be a source of emotional and financial support upon your release. Friends and family can provide places to live, meals, referrals for jobs, transportation, and someone to talk to. Family can provide all that friendship provides, plus help in areas where you need a higher level of trust, like co-signing for a car or a place to live. Family can be added to your checking and savings accounts. Family can be given powers of attorney to handle taxes, investment, and legal issues, all while you are in or out of custody.

So now you may want to stop and review quadrant III again, think of family members, friends, business associates once more. Write down and note all of them. **Now, while in cus-**

tody, start to apologize, start to get humble, and start developing strong personal relations again from the inside. You may need to swallow your pride. Do not let your ego take over. This is a time to be humble, honest, and giving. Attending religious services can help with the humility and thankfulness required. As you continue reading this book, you will find out that your personal network or friends, family, and business are one of the most valuable assets you own. If you have a trade, you will be way ahead of the game. And later I will show you how to turn your trade into gold. Once you feel your relationships have improved to where you can count on them for something (home, shelter, food, transportation, consolation, or financial support), add them to your asset list.

2. **Unclaimed Property:** You were arrested and thought you lost track of everything. You think that $50 left in a savings bank years ago is now lost. But guess what: All is not lost! California's Unclaimed Property Law requires corporations, businesses, associations, financial institutions, and insurance companies (referred to as "Holders") to annually report and deliver property to the California State Controller's Office after there has been no activity on the account or contact with the owner for a period of time specified in the law - generally (3) three years or more. Do you have an unused gift card, a bank account you

forgot about, a credit balance in a retail store? I personally forgot about a credit balance I had at Guitar Center for $100, and I found an auto insurance premium refund for $128. And sure enough, when I went to the website for California Unclaimed Property (https://ucpi.sco.ca.gov) and ran the search, and there were several accounts. A bank account with $50, a credit card with a credit balance for returned items that I had just forgotten about, etc. Finding money post-custody is like gold— rare and precious. If you had money coming to you, but because you were arrested, they just can't find you, odds are the money is being held by the State. Here are some of the most common types of unclaimed property:

- Bank Accounts
- Safe Deposit Contents
- Stocks and Bonds and Dividends
- Un-Cashed Cashier Checks and Money Orders
- Matured or Terminated Insurance Policies

You don't have to wait for your release. You can get started on it now with the help of your friends or family members. It is a great way to start nurturing a new fresh-start relationship with them as well. Make the phone call or write the letter to your family or friends, ask them to check it out for you. At the same time, ask them to put money on the phone, so you can call them. Plan your call and make that 15 minutes valuable. Lastly, the unclaimed property system is now very high tech.

You can find your claim, and if the money is available, you can do it all online and get the return of your property within 14 days! This money is a blessing.

3. **The Saddleback Church and the PEACE Center ministries**. This is almost a one-stop-shop for recovery. Plus, you have the added benefit of either establishing or re-establishing your faith. I can not say enough about Saddleback Church. God has built an organization that can and will change your life forever and can give you purpose. I had the honor and the privilege of volunteering at their food pantry, which is a major part of the Peace Center in the City of Lake Forest in Orange County, California. The food pantry can and will gladly share 3-5 days of groceries until you're back on your feet. Most importantly, all of their ministries are an open invitation to return to God. Joanne, Amanda, Will, and Kamron are some of the kindest souls you will ever meet on this planet, and they know that getting you back on the right track is very important in God's eyes.

Never Give Up! You can always return back to God no matter how far you have strayed. The people at Saddleback Church can help you to become truly devoted and close to God. The best way to explore Saddleback Church is to either personally make a visit to the PEACE Center or visit them online at www.saddleback.com. Take the time to review all the outreach programs and care ministries. They do have a ministry for families with loved ones in custody. There is no reason why your family has to wait for your release. The church is also a source for legal and tax advice. Have your family members contact the church now, while you are in custody, and research all services they provide. This is another way to start working together with your family and friends. Take baby steps to build that new life, even though right now, you are still behind bars.

The Celebrate Recovery Program is a program founded by one of the ministers at Saddleback Church. Its Purpose Statement is to help people find freedom from hurts, habits, and hang-ups, including addictions, compulsive, and dysfunctional behaviors. The Saddleback Church is an asset you will want to participate with either directly or indirectly, whether you live near the church or not. You can always participate online by going to www.saddleback.com/watch. There are thousands of Celebrate Recovery groups around the world, including inside. There are groups inside that study *The Purpose Driven Life* and *What on Earth am I Here For?* This church is a huge asset. Now add it to your asset list.

4. **California Lifeline Phone.** With unlimited talk, text, and internet, there isn't a better deal anywhere, and it's free for those in need. You will need either a State Benefits Card (BIC), which is issued to you upon your release, or a Califor-

nia Advantage Card (EBT), which is provided under the Food Stamp SNAP program through your county's social services program. Getting this phone will be one of the first things you will want to do. What could be more important than conserving your money and having a phone? This allows you to reach out to friends, family, potential employers, or research items on the internet. If you're starting with $200 gate money, this is a big-time asset.

5. **California Snap Program CalFresh** (Federally known as the Supplemental Nutrition Assistance Program or SNAP). This is a federally mandated, state-supervised, and county-operated government entitlement program that provides monthly food benefits to assist low-income households in purchasing the food they need to maintain adequate nutritional levels. Let's face it, when you get out of prison, you will have $200. And, if you don't plan in advance, you'll have no job. That's about as low-income as it gets. In general, these benefits are for any food or food product intended for human consumption. This can add to your food budget to put healthy and nutritious food on the table. At one time, it could only be used to purchase uncooked food, but now some restaurants are offering complete meals using the EBT. If you are finding it difficult to afford the nutritious food that you and your family needs, the CalFresh Program will be able to help you. Most

people released from prison are automatically qualified. The amount of benefits you can receive depends on your family size, countable income, and monthly expenses such as housing, utilities, and so forth. All U.S. citizens or Legal Permanent Resident children may qualify to receive CalFresh benefits, regardless of where the parents were born. Parents may also be eligible for benefits if all other program guidelines are met. Individuals with no children also may qualify. The program issues monthly benefits that can be used to buy most foods in many markets and food stores. These benefits are issued on an Electronic Benefits Transfer (EBT) card, which looks like any other credit card. You do not have to be on welfare to get CalFresh benefits. Eligibility for CalFresh assistance, as well as the benefit amount, is based on your household's size and income level. Benefits may not be used for items such as alcoholic beverages, cigarettes, or paper products.

The EBT option is another topic that can be explored by friends and family while you're in custody. The typical monthly amount is $192/month and is enough for one person to live for a month if you plan correctly. Without spending a lot of time, you can protect your gate money by buying your food with your EBT card at places like Grocery Outlet, Aldi, or Ralphs. If you combine that with a conservative shopping list, you're going to be good for the month easily. This is another huge asset during your transition to freedom. But be forewarned, these entitlement programs are only *temporary* assets and are not to be considered permanent assets. Take every month you receive the benefit with the greatest of gratitude to your Creator. It's a blessing He is providing for you, but He also expects you to live a productive life. It's a two-way street. Once you reach a point where it is not needed anymore, let it go. Don't wait until they tell you you're not qualified anymore. Let the next person in line receive their blessing. That's doing the right thing.

6. **California General Relief:** The General Assistance or General Relief (GA/GR) Program is designed to provide relief and support to indigent adults who are not supported by their own means, other public funds, or assistance programs. Each county's GA/GR program is established and funded (100%) by its own Board of Supervisors. As the State is not involved in this program, benefits, payment levels, and eligibility requirements will vary among each of California's 58 counties. For further information or to apply for the GA/GR Program, either you or your family need to contact your county social services agency. Many, if not all, of the GA/GR recipients are also eligible to participate in the CalFresh Program that we just mentioned. Keep in mind, though, the CalFresh Program is specifically designed to raise the level of nutrition among low-income households.

To apply for GA/GR and/or CalFresh benefits, contact your county social services agency. The GA/GR program should only be used for a very temporary period, such as the first few months after release, and should be avoided, if possible. This is a very time consuming and depressing process. If you have to bite the bullet, do it. I hope that you have learned enough from this book to have something planned upon your exit. If you do not, this is another temporary asset to tap, with a strong emphasis on **temporary**.

7. **California Protected Status:** On January 1, 2018, California's ban-the-box law took effect. Amendments to California's Fair Housing and Employment Act (FEHA) make it illegal for private and public employers with five or more employees to ask about criminal history until the later stages of the application process. The purpose of the law is to encourage employers to assess each applicant's fitness for the job, rather than categorically deny employment to those with a criminal past. In California, convicted felons have been given protective status. This means that, as of now, you are no longer required to share your felony status with prospective employers, and employers are not permitted to ask upfront. Potential employers do get around it by saying it is part of the hiring process, but you have the right to decline. Then they ask you to volunteer the information. But in many cases, when the labor market is tight,

some employers are willing not to look too deep. My personal experience has been nothing short of terrible. I believe the real reason is that I have both the felony and the age factor working against me. But it's only been 110 days since I crossed the gate to freedom. When I did cross that bridge, my financial plan called for prioritizing my health check-ups first. Over the past three years in Fire Camp, we never had a doctor visit. Also, at age 66, I'm eligible for Social Security, so that also took priority. In actuality, it's been maybe 60 days of hard job hunting. That is why it is essential while you are in custody to nurture your relationships with friends and family so they can help you find possible employment. On the 115th day of freedom, and after approximately 70 days of job hunting, things started to click! I started work. I want to share more of this in detail. Toward the end of this book, I plan to share my job search journey so that you can learn from my mistakes.

The Short Version: The bottom line is that California Protected Status is an Asset. Don't volunteer your criminal history to an employer or a landlord unless asked directly. Do share your criminal history and information with your bank and with your doctors.

I hope that these assets were eye-openers for you. They were for me today. This is my 283rd day of freedom. In 5 days, I will receive my SNAP payment of $192. My daughter is picking me up this Sunday to go shopping at Trader Joes. In 2 days, I get my next paycheck, and in 8 days, my Social Security checking account and will hit the $5,000 **"E" Fund mark.** This all started with $200 and no place to live. Have faith in God, and He will provide for you. Every day, work at placing your trust in God. There is no one else besides Him. Who else should you really place all your trust in? So, do your goal setting and get a plan in motion. Don't expect things to change overnight, but do reflect back on your accomplishments every day. It really helps to keep you focused on your goals and getting through the bad days and hard times.

Liabilities you may not have considered:
1. **Mental State** - Now that we have discussed the *Assets* you may not have thought of, let's look at the *Liabilities*. Liabilities are pretty straight forward; they are things for which someone is responsible, especially a debt or financial obligation, things you owe. There are a few important things to note here. Don't be afraid or stress out over your liabilities. They are one of those things that can make you dysfunctional, as we discussed earlier under the subject title "Why do people fail." And while we are on that subject of your mental state, sometimes it gets really depressing when you start thinking way too far down the line. Liabilities can really do you in. Sometimes you can't see the light at the end of the tunnel. It can get really depressing and make you feel really

apprehensive. Planning too far down the road is just not realistic— especially upon your release. Things are changing really quickly, and your mind needs to catch up to the speed of the real world. There's nothing wrong with being a little stressed out. Just try and stay calm and open-minded during the planning stages. If you find yourself feeling too uncomfortable, take a break and come back to it later.

You will need to commit everything you're thinking about to paper. You should be mentally focused daily on the here and now. It's also a good idea to reflect back on daily accomplishments. For each day that goes by, if you can and have paper and something to write with, it's a great idea to journal your time reflecting on your daily accomplishments. Then, reviewing your journal later will further encourage you. It can also be used as a reference tool to look back and see why "that day was a bad day." For every day, whether inside or outside of custody, I have a list of daily to-do's. And I always have my sheet of longer-term goals nearby. The daily list leads to the other, longer-term goals. So don't stress out if you have substantial liabilities. More importantly, while you are in custody, do your best to identify them. What you don't want is surprises! So, if you are unsure of what your liabilities are, you can ask friends and family to assist you. Are your taxes up to date? If not, you can contact the IRS for transcripts. If you have money owed to people, consider your relationship with those people. If you owe corporations, you want to identify those corporations. Credit card companies can be contacted and informed that you are in custody. It's better than just letting it go. And lastly, try to find out if you have any judgments outstanding.

Child support is probably the most aggressive of them all. This is an area that needs to be addressed upfront, not as a surprise. Child support administrative actions wield a lot of power, such as the power to garnish wages, place a lien property, withhold your passport, and offset your personal income tax refunds. Try to be very as proactive as you can about child support. If possible, come together and try to resolve the issues with whoever is caring for your child, wife, girlfriend, etc. Now take a moment and write down your liabilities.

2. **Reputation** - Unlike the multitude of potential hidden assets, liabilities, for the most part, are pretty straight forward. But there are a few that are not as obvious. One liability that is sometimes not considered as a liability is "reputation." it's a real deal when you're trying to rehabilitate and merge back into society. It's not an easy fix unless you are suddenly found not guilty, and they take that mistake public. There are rare cases, but you have to be really lucky even if you are not guilty and behind bars in error. Face it, no one wants

to admit a mistake, and even though courtrooms have that statue of Blind Justice, you know and I know that is not the case. You are guilty from the beginning and have to prove that you are innocent. So, just like a financial liability, energy is needed to reduce this liability of "Reputation." One of the ways to offset a marred reputation is volunteering. Volunteering can substantially reduce a bad reputation. Doing acts of kindness, even though you will be getting something in return, people take notice. It's your intention that matters most here. Generosity should be given the Lord's way. "A Generous Heart Gives Freely." If you plan to change your life, you need to unlock new doors, and the key to unlocking those doors is doing kind acts and giving charity. Remember also that charity doesn't have to be in the form of money. You can share your time, your energy, and your possessions. You can just open your heart and give a caring response to someone in need of another. Do this, and surely your reputation will be rebuilt again. Get this: you don't have to wait until you are released. Right now, look around at the people standing right next to you. Certainly, there's someone in need of a helping hand or someone to listen to what they have to say. It's a blessing. Get started. Start changing. It gets habit-forming.

3. **Location** - Location can be a major liability. If you come from a high-crime neighborhood with prior neighborhood connections into illegal activities,

you are going to want to be as far away from this area as possible. Your family and friends can help here. The unfortunate part is that you must stay in your county when on parole or probation. But you can bite the bullet and plan for your new life in another location with new friends and a lower crime rate.

4. **Becoming Institutionalized** - Realize that the California Prison System is big business, and it's natural for those working for the system to be interested in keeping their jobs and providing for their families. It's interesting to note that all the cities surrounding the prisons have very high crime rates. So much so that it has become an expected part of daily life. I was recently in a Fresno County Sunday church service, where they talked about prisons and incarceration as if it was just another social group that the church helps. "Who's baking cookies for the inmates this week? What about a toy drive for the children whose parents are in prison?" You need to know that being in custody is not in any way, shape, or form the norm. It's not a life— no matter how comfortable the conditions may be, especially in Fire Camp. Just because your parents made mistakes and found themselves behind bars doesn't mean you have to follow their lead and go to prison, too. This is not college. There is no learning here.

While in Jamestown, I overheard two older inmates talking about their retirement strategy.

Here's what they said: "If a person has no family left, no money, and no home, then the best thing to do is walk into a bank with a note saying this is a stick-up. That will get you some Federal Prison Time, where the accommodations are great!" I've personally witnessed inmates being so completely satisfied with prison life and Fire Camp, that they were hugging the trees, so they didn't have to leave on their release dates. Why? Because during fire seasons, the meals are ramped up to 5000 calories per day for the firefighters, and the in-campers get to join in. Steak, shrimp, ice cream, cake, and candy! These in-campers are not like the firefighters. In-campers don't work very hard. They do minimal tasks, like picking up pieces of paper on the floor. They take pride in not doing much of anything all day if they can. These in-campers become totally satisfied with camp life. It's a major liability. Don't get used to it. Custody is not where you want to be. You are only feeding a system that is already way too big. This book will show you how to make a decent life for yourself. You may not have a choice right now, so use your time wisely and study, pray, get smart, and use this book to *get out and stay out*!

CHAPTER 5

Creating Your Personal Roadmap to Success

At this point, many students/readers revert back to their goal maps and redefine their priorities. Go do that. Go back and dial it in. You have just learned a ton of new information. Once you have made your changes, it's time to start creating your plan. In this section, I've shared so many of my thoughts and observations over the past 3½ years in custody. I've done this to share my point of view, but don't expect it to be your point of view. No need to agree or disagree. You should be designing a plan based upon your values, the goals you have established, their importance to you, and the priority you assigned them to. But do realize that I have experienced much of this first hand. There's nothing wrong with using what been established for you.

You will need to deal with all emergencies first. I know that I just covered this topic in the previous chapter, but these are so important they need to be addressed again. Emergencies like substance abuse or psychological problems, if you have them, need to be resolved. You will not be able to function in a free environment if you're craving a substance or thinking about hurting yourself or others. Those need to be your first priorities, so start dealing with them now. Don't wait, talk to your counselor now! Ask about participating in a program upon release, and, if you have long-term substance abuse issues, look for longer-term programs and not the shorter ones. Learn from the experiences of other inmates. Those three-month programs don't do much to help at all. If you have no other options, take it. It's better than nothing. You can also check out your prison or jail library to research programs. Reach out to your lawyer or counselor for the possibility of being alternatively sentenced with psychological care. The bottom line is you cannot facilitate a financial plan (or life plan for that matter) when your priorities are not in order. Don't even think about being a working addict. *It will catch up with you.* Look at your goal maps. How many of you wrote in Quadrant I (Personal Goals): "the need to remove substance from my life" A-1 (Emergency Priority 1)? If you did, again, I say, my hat is off to you. But without looking over your shoulder, my guess the first thing you listed was to get a job or make money. If you want to return to custody, don't take my advice, put the book away, and forget it, and thank you for your purchase. If you do not get your priorities straight, you will be released and back on the street, either selling or doing drugs to survive. Once you're back into your routine, it's just a matter of time until law enforcement catches up with you. If you think I'm just taking off on the subject, you are absolutely right. In Fire Camp, I met in-campers and firefighters going on their sixth prison term. In Jamestown, there were guys on their ninth and tenth prison term. All of them had one thing in common: "substance abusers." During one Sunday church service at Jamestown, there was a minister (a free man who served five terms in Jamestown Prison) who told the fellowship that it took him five terms in prison to finally come to the conclusion that he had to quit using drugs. It was simple. It wasn't complicated at all. He told us that since quitting drugs, he has never been behind bars since. It's not rocket science here. That's why getting clean and staying clean is an A=Emergency 1! This is your first priority.

If you are using drugs in prison, you need to do everything possible to stop. If that means changing your location into a different dorm or cell, find a reason without ratting anyone out, and just do it. I changed my dorm in Jamestown. I was living next to six addicts, and it wasn't pretty. I lived in this dorm for several months, and all of them were up all night and using the same needle. One gent was transferred to a Fire Camp. Another gent had a bad reaction to whatever he was sticking in his arm and went into seizures one night. He survived but was sent to another prison. On my right, the guy on the upper bed was sent back to court for another case. He was at risk of getting another 4 years. The guy on the lower bunk ran up a huge drug debt. He walked out into a mob who started to beat the crap out of him. He got away only to find another group pouncing on him. He was finally removed from the A yard (Lowest Level Yards) and placed into a protective custody cell. All of this is related to drug use, even in prison! It's really bad. The guy across from me was 60 plus years old and on his 9th prison term. If you are at risk, first, you have to accept the situation. Don't rat anyone out, just be strong and avoid using substances at all costs. That includes Pruno and Tobacco. Get used to not having to need anything other than God, health, food, water, and exercise. Get high on life!

Let's Get Started With Some Plan Building Help

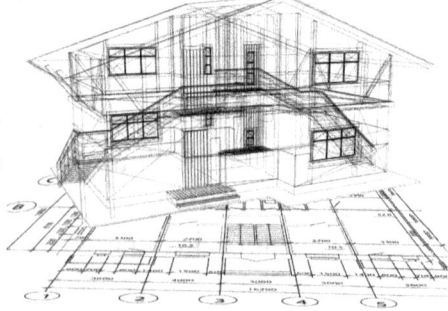

We need to start somewhere, so let's begin by starting with writing down basics to get this going. Try to use a separate writing pad. Purchase one either through the commissary, package, or canteen. Or have a family member mail a few writing pads to you. The preference is to buy them through the institution so that you have the cardboard backing. When my family would send writing pads in the mail, the guards would rip the cardboard from the back of the pads. Try to get several pads so you can re-write the plan again and again, always learning and always improving.

So let's begin by writing down some of your personal information. I've included a little commentary in each section to help.

- First Name
- Last Name (Your name used should be your legal name and not your moniker "prison name")
- Birthdate
- Age
- Marital Status
- SS#
- Employer
- Occupation/Trade
- Address (Use your last known for your address and employer)
    - Street
    - City
    - Postal Code

- ☐ Cell Phone
- ☐ Home Phone
- ☐ Work Phone
- ☐ Your Email Address
- ☐ Spouse's Name
- ☐ Spouse's Address
- ☐ Spouse's Work Phone
- ☐ Spouse's Email Address
- ☐ Dependents
  - First Name, Last Name, Birthdate, Age
- ☐ Wills
  - Do you have a will? Yes No
  - Date of last update
  - Notes:
- ☐ Do you have a Trust? Yes No
  - Date of last update
- ☐ Life Insurance
  - Policy Type
  - Company
  - Insured
  - Coverage Amount
- ☐ Advisors
  - Financial advisor(s)
  - Lawyer(s)
  - Accountant(s)
  - Insurance agent(s)
  - Friends Considered

If listing your basic information triggers a new goal, such as to create a will or trust for your family, go back and add it in on your goal list under personal goals. Then assign it a priority and a number for importance.

You want to make your plan to be as realistic as possible. These are not perfect documents. There are a lot of estimates and assumptions. Take a look at the following sample disclaimer used in the professional financial planning industry:

> *The figures stated in the plan are all derived based on assumptions and information provided by you, the reader/user. These assumptions and information will change over time. Some of the information presented is based on current tax rules and legislation which are subject to change. Hence, it is imperative that you review your financial plan regularly to ensure it is up-to-date and addresses your current needs. It is also important to look at a few different scenarios to get an idea of the impact of various assumptions on your planning objectives.*

That is another big mouthful. But we can learn a lot from that paragraph even though you are creating your own plan. Most of the time, the disclaimer's purpose is used as a risk reduction tool for the financial planning firm. What we can learn from this is that financial planning and developing financial plans are an on-going process and not a quick fix—even after you have created it. It's in your best interest to review it every 3 or 4 months to see if you need to make any changes. Changes in tax laws and other laws can have a direct effect on your financial plan. In reality, you should know your plan so well that eventually, you will make it a part of your daily life. On the other hand, and more importantly, don't worry about making it perfect. It is more important to get an imperfect plan down on paper and continuously improve it. That is the real key to the process.

Your financial plan should flow in order. Remember the big six? Cash flow, risk management, tax planning, saving and investment planning, future planning, and estate planning. That order is what is generally used. I do not believe there is any specific rule. I have seen, on occasion, tax planning and risk management written towards the end of the financial plan. That makes sense as well. But remember, the main focus of this book is Cash Flow and Risk Management, not preclude you from addressing the other four. That's entirely up to you.

You may not think of yourself as a writer, and you really don't have to be one. You just need to write a sentence, and it doesn't even need to be a proper one. As long as you understand it, that's all that matters. So if you weren't the A student in your English class, "Who cares?" Getting the ideas down on paper is the most important thing to be concerned with.

Need Help Creating Those Sentences? Think Who, What, Where, When, Why, How and How Much

Answering the question of **Who, What, Where, When, Why, How** and **How Much** will help you create the sentences and thoughts for your financial plan. Let's use an example from Quadrant I of our chart: "Eat healthiest possible diet B1". By the way, this is really an important personal goal, but a really tough one to deal with when in custody. From my experience, the Kosher meals were the healthiest, and you don't have to be Jewish. Let's get back to forming the sentences and using our example.

Who: you

What: eating a healthy diet

Where: in jail, prison, out on parole

When: now, next week, next month

Why: maintaining a healthy diet is part of living a healthy lifestyle so that I will be able to enjoy the fruits of my planning. This is common sense. Why go through all of this and then get sick and not able to enjoy it?

How: research healthy diets at the Prison Library, requesting information from family and friends, study from the internet, or ask your doctor, either in custody or upon your release.

Here's a sample statement that represents what I just detailed above:

I want to start to eat a more healthy diet. I need to check it out online, at the library, or ask my family and friends to send me information. Or I can also make an appointment to see the prison/jail doctor/nurse practitioner and request the best diet for my age, weight, and lifestyle. I can start working on this right now. That's it!

Let's try another example: Start a business.
Who: you, unless your considering partners then it would be you and whomever
What: start my "Auto Detailing Business"
Where: your county
When: within 6 months of my release
Why: I need to generate X amount per month
How: Social Media and network with family and friends
How Much: you fill in the blanks

Here's a sample statement that represents what I just detailed above:

I want to start an Auto Detailing Business with my friend Jack within 6 months of my release. Orange County has an enormous amount of high-end vehicles, and there is a huge demand for detailing work. We plan to advertise on social media and go to industrial parks and offer executives and business owners the service while the cars are parked during the day. Jack has a truck and all the equipment. If successful, we will far exceed the X amount that

I need to have a comfortable standard of living according to my expenses.

You should start getting a feel for how to write these. If not, just go for it and change it up the next day. Even if it sounds corny, just do it. If you need more help or have questions, write to us at the address located in the back reference guide.

Here's Some More Help

Planning For A Place To Stay

Considerations For The Critical First Sixth Months

Go to your current status, "the motion picture," which is the cash flow money in and money out. Total up just the absolute necessities, the absolute rock bottom things you will need upon your release during the first six months. Once you have that number, write it in Quadrant II B1: "I'm going to need X amount per month for the first six months." Now, let's attempt to tear that number all the way down to the bare bones.

The first six months is your most critical time. If you're starting with just $200 gate money and you need a place to stay, your goal is to develop strong enough relationships with family or friends to have that place until you get yourself established. You should try and begin this process as soon as possible.

Do not wait until you are released. Get on the phone or start writing letters. You can write letters without envelopes or money on the book by requesting indigent envelopes and postage, which are provided by the prisons at no cost. It's also vital not to prejudge the responses from your family and friends. Simply ask and be prepared for a "no." Remember, a "no" today can become a "maybe" tomorrow. Really be humble if you get a "yes." There are two times in your life when people will go over and above to support you personally. The first is when and if you are released from prison or jail. The other is when you're starting a new business. Let's not forget that for someone to open their home to you (a felon) is a big deal. They need to feel safe and have a high level of trust. It's so essential to put in the time and energy to build those relationship bridges as soon as possible. You do all that you can do, and the rest is in the hands of God. If you have exhausted all of the other options and you still don't have a place to go, then the next step is to fill out a California CDCR Form C-22. Request a meeting with your counselor to see if they have any transition programs for you. You can also ask the same of your probation officer, once outside the gate. But that means you may be spending a cold night on a park bench until you meet your probation officer the following morning.

The other alternatives are the county and city missions, such as LA County Rescue Mission or The Orange County Mission. There are missions everywhere. We will discuss this in more detail later. If you know you will not have a place to stay when you get out, go to the prison or jail library now or have a family member or friend do some research online. Find these locations in the county you are paroling to and write to them in advance. Develop the same relationship you would with family. Start writing and find a place to stay. You do not want to use your gate money for a cheap motel room. Do everything you can to avoid that.

Now write it out: Upon my release, I'm planning to live with my Aunty Ann and hope that I can live there for at least the first six months.

Moving on to money and how to help you develop Your Monthly Cash Flow Goal for the first six months. Let's take a look at the total estimated costs of the five major expenses I list below. Please do not concern yourself about making money at this point in the process. It is more important to make a list of what you absolutely need. Then you can work on how to make money.

First Six Months

A good guesstimate for **housing** expense would be somewhere between $500-$2000 per month. But don't stress out. If you have done your homework and did a good job building those relationships, you can take advantage of your one-time release card with family or friends. Or you may use a prison or county transition program or your local Mission. So, hopefully, you will spend **nothing.**

In absence of a program, your **food** will cost between $200-$500 per month. But if you have done your homework, the plan is to take advantage of the assets of your family or friends, a prison or county transition program, or local Mission. If so, you will spend **nothing (plus at this point, you can apply for the Cal-Fresh "Snap" Food Stamp Program).** That program will provide around $192.00 per month that you can spend on groceries (but not alcohol, paper goods, or tobacco products). We get into more detail about this later, but for right now, write down the estimate you think you will need for food and groceries. Hopefully, you will spend **nothing.**

Your **medical insurance** expenses ordinarily would run approximately $100-$200 monthly. When you are released from prison, you are automatically on probation or parole (either way) for a minimum of a year to a maximum of three years, depending on your crime. Technically, you are still in custody, and they do provide medical care until you are formally released from parole or probation. By the way, when you are released, you receive paperwork from your parole officers, which gives you the date when you will be off parole if you have no violations. Make sure to get your release paperwork. You don't want to find out that you're still on parole because they forgot to process your paperwork. If you're not on parole or probation, medical insurance should be provided by your transitional program. If you don't have either of those, head to a Mission and participate in their program. Or you can just march on over to the Saddleback Peace Center Medical Clinic. They never refuse anyone regardless of financial issues. The net cost of medical insurance for the first six months should be **nothing**, but make sure to write down what your medical needs are in your plan. Some of you may have special medical needs, and the rules change all the time.

A monthly **clothing** expense allowance of $200 is being very realistic. You're probably going to have to rebuild your wardrobe. Hope and pray that the relationships with family and friends that you are attempting to revive prosper and that they will be there to help you out. If not, the Salvation Army Family Store can really help you here. The 2019 pricing for a Sports Jacket suitable for job interviews run $15 or less. A pair of jeans is $5-8. They have shoes, T-shirts, everything you need to get back on your feet. You may have to spend some of your precious gate money. Try to hold off as long as possible, but you can get two-days' worth of clothing for under **$25.00**. Write down what you think you need for clothing into your plan.

Communication & Internet is a critical expense. In reality, you should purchase the best phone and best service available if given the opportunity. This is your lifeline, your gateway to getting a job. This is how you will stay in touch with loved ones, maintaining and building critical relationships. This is your gateway to the information highway. Expect to pay $100 per month for this worth-while, essential tool. This is hard without a job and only $200 in your pocket. The State/Federal government provides Lifeline Phone. It will give you unlimited calling, unlimited texting, and access to the Internet. You will spend **nothing**. Write down your communication and internet needs into your plan.

Plan on **transportation** expense of $300, which would include the cost of a financed car, maintenance, gas, and insurance. You're not riding high. You're just riding. Transportation means owning a car for most of us in this country. If you have a car, that's one thing. If your friends or family are willing to provide a car, that's another thing. But if you do not have the money or the resources to purchase a car, forget it. Check out public transportation or, my personal favorite, just walk. Try to situate yourself where you can access everything you need just by walking. It's healthy to walk. You can plan or think. And it's a great way to pray. If you need to get your driver's license renewed, by all means, do so. You will find it will take you two months to get an appointment at the DMV, or you can stand in line for 5 hours. With only $200 in your pocket, walking is just the right thing to do. The next best thing is the bus system. Let me share what I did, I walked almost everywhere for the first two months. Then, I started to use the bus occasionally for the third month. By the fourth month, I did find a job, opened a bank account, and was able to rent a car for a few days a month to take care of errands that required a car. So, if you followed me on this, if given a choice I walked. If needed to go further, I checked out the bus system and used them only if I had to. Then I would combine things to do and rent a car for the day. I know this one is hard. But unless you have resources, the first 6 months is not the time or place to spend money on automobiles when you don't have to. Remember also that 99% of all police confrontations occur in the automobile. You don't want police confrontations because once they ask for ID, you really have no choice but to tell them you are on parole or probation. While on the subject, if you do have a police confrontation of any sort, even if it is not a hostile experience, you need to pick up up the phone and tell your parole/probation officer immediately. If they not available, you should leave a voice mail to cover your butt. These people do not like surprises of any kind.

Now with what you have just learned, start writing out what you want to accomplish within the first six months out of custody. Look at all your goals, consider your resources, and write out your plan. Remember, you must always maintain a positive cash flow. Use the Who, What, Where, When, Why, How and How Much formula to create each statement. There is no limit on the number of statements you can make. In Quadrant II, plugin your X for the first six months. Here's what it potentially can look like:

Expenses:

Food √	$192 EBT
Family/ Friends/ Grocery Outlet, Aldi	
Rent √	$0
Laundry at Laundromat √	$ 20
Public Transportation √	$100
Family/Friends, Walking, Bus, Car Rentals	
Auto Payment	
Auto Insurance	
Auto Gas	
Auto Maintenance	
Cell Phone (use LifeLine Phone) √	$0
Personal Care (Haircut) √	$ 20
Medical √	Out of pocket
Entertainment/Internet √	Use cell phone
Clothing (Salvation Army) √	$25
Home Improvement	
Vacation	
Gifts	
Charity √	Donate your time

The Next Period: Six to Eighteen Months

The next phase or benchmark occurs around the sixth-month mark and is estimated to last until the eighteenth month. But please remember this will be different for everyone. It is assumed that you have found a job by now and that your income has exceeded your basic six-month necessity expenses. With your positive cash flow and an accumulation discipline, it's now time to build in some risk management tools and protect what you accumulated. First and foremost, you should build the "Emergency Fund" with an initial target amount of $5000. You should consider in your mind, that until you have that $5000, you are dead flat broke. I was able to accomplish this within 10 months. Other students/inmates that I worked with took 12 months to accumulate $5000. Some of the luckier inmates who worked in Fire Camp and didn't spend a penny of their very hard-earned firefighting money on packages, shoes, and electronics, walked out of prison with $5000. But remember, out of the approximate 180,000 inmates in the State Prison System, only around 4000 inmates get a chance to work in Fire Camp. You may ask why $5000. That's a great question, and I'm glad you asked it. Sixty percent of millennials would have to beg, borrow, or steal right at this moment if confronted with a mere $1000 in emergency expenses. This is according to a new survey (http://ghepublishing.com/LendingTree) from LendingTree, which defines the generation as those between 22 and 37 in age. But the rest of the country doesn't fare much better. Only 42% of Gen-X could come up with a $1000 to cover an emergency, and

just 60% of the Boomers. The other percentage said they'd either
- borrow from family or friends (16%),
- sell something or use a credit card (9% each),
- work more (7%), or
- take out a loan (6%).

These are very sad but true figures, considering that these numbers pertain to free working individuals.

Traditional professional financial planning has used a rule of thumb that you need to hold at least 6 months of your fixed expenses in cash— liquid and readily available to be used if needed for an emergency. This is called an Emergency fund or Contingency fund. Let's save some keystrokes on the keyboard and just call it The E Fund. It's very important for many reasons.

Back to the question of why—and there are many reasons. First of all, to create this fund requires the discipline to save. You must learn to save and not let the money in your pocket burn a hole in your pants. You may think this is funny, but it's not. From every direction, from the instant you wake up, you are bombarded with advertising that tries to make you feel that life will be better with some new product or service that you need to buy *right now*! It's out of control! With companies like Amazon, who employ artificial intelligence to learn everything they can about you, and the power of Black Friday and Cyber Monday, you need the force to be with you!

Darth Vader is out there wanting to reach in and take everything you have. And Darth could give a rat's ass about you. These companies don't care if you are successful, rich/poor, happy/sad, healthy/unhealthy... they just want to separate you from your hard-earned money. As OB Wan Kenobe would say, "You Need To Feel The Force, Luke." That's what's really going on. Every minute of the day, there's a Dark Side that attacks you and attempts to separate you from your money. Watches, cars, cell phones. Carefully crafted words, internet videos, and television commercials all pounding at you from all sides to let it go. "Don't be a cheapskate, stop watching your buck."

I counseled lots of very wealthy clients. Most of them have inherited their wealth or won it in a lawsuit or married into it. Very few have become wealthy on their own by working very hard. But I can tell you this that the ones that did work hard for it share one big thing in common. They could care less about commercials, or what other people have. They are focused on saving and watching every penny. They spend only with purpose. That purpose could be a gift, a super vacation, or simply not spending at all. They are in control, not the commercials.

You need to be stubborn to give up a buck. Always think about how to avoid spending money today. Enjoy the great feeling of money accumulating in your possession. Right now, it's the time to live like a total miser until you reach $5000. And that's just the beginning. Don't even concern yourself with making money on your money yet. The most important part of this $5000 is that it be at arms reach and available to you all the time without penalty. I can tell you from personal experience, the day you hit that $5000, especially when you started out with just $200 gate money, it is a really, really good feeling. You are thankful to God for the great accomplishment. You did it, and you should be proud of yourself. From now on, moving forward, you are no longer dead flat broke!

So, where do you keep this money? If you do not owe money to the State or Federal government, child support, or other pending judgments, you can keep it in a savings account with internet access or a checking account. If you do have child support payments, IRS, or any other possible creditors lurking or breathing down your back, I have three words for you "CASH IS KING!" And before you ask where should you keep $5000 cash, here are a few suggestions: You can keep the cash on your person all the times with a money belt available at most travel stores. 50 one hundred dollar bills take up a surprisingly small space. You can buy a home safe available at Costco, Target, or Walmart. They run anywhere from $29-$100. Then you can use $5's, $10's and $20's if you like. I also suggest that if you are going to use smaller bills, get some free cash envelopes from the bank. Pack each envelope with $1000. This way, there is no need to stress out when you are counting your money. You already know that you have 5 envelopes with $1000 in each one.

Don't worry about making a 2% return. There is no gambling permitted at this point. This is an emergency fund. Don't even think about using it to buy a car. You're going to just hold on to it. Learn how to make plenty of money with this $5000 by just holding on to it. I'm going to show you how shortly.

Please take a moment and pause from your reading because it's important for you to write into your plan the estimated time you expect to meet the E Fund Goal. As we discussed at the beginning of the book and in this section, once you have achieved a positive cash flow, the positive cash flow itself becomes a valuable asset and needs to be protected. Here are the exact words from the first section: *If you have more money coming in than going out, you have a positive Cash Flow (Cash Flow Planning). It's worth something and, therefore, an asset, a very valuable asset that needs to be protected. (Risk Planning).* If you remember, we said that we have many ways to manage risk. One way was to *accept* the risk; one way was to *avoid* the risk; another way was to *reduce* the risk; and the last way was to *transfer* the risk to a third party (most of the time, that's an insurance company). Consider your $5000 E Fund as a way of being able to accept risk— like your own self-insurance fund. You can and should accept certain risks. There is a lot of benefit to having an E Fund.

So while we are on the subject, let's start with the obvious, with your E Fund, you are no longer living hand to mouth. This is huge. If you have an issue with your new employer and you have to leave abruptly, which becomes and unplanned-smack-in-the-face emergency, you're not on the street that night. You have a cushion to soften the blow. How many people live with abusive employment situations simply because they do not have money to fall back on? Don't think your employer doesn't know it. Small business owners have a special talent for sniffing out if you are totally dependent on the job for survival. *They Know*. You don't want to be in that position ever again. You can do that with an E Fund.

Let's move on. Sometime within the next 12 months, you will want to buy some electronics: Phone, TV, Toaster, or a Coffee Maker. This is part of the home expense category on the prepared expense list (Motion Picture). You have your E Fund. You have money left over. The job is good. So you decide you're going to buy a big-screen TV. You have it in your cart. You're feeling good— excited to get home and set it up. Right at the checkout, the Dark Side appears, and Darth Vader will now drill you to buy the extended warranty or insurance to guard against the damage or loss of your purchase. But now, Luke Skywalker is here—your E Fund! With total confidence, you can just say, "NO THANK YOU" because the Force is with you. You've got E Fund Self Insurance. Some of these contracts for extended warranty cost $50 to $80. Others, like Cell Phone insurance, are charging $10-$15 dollars per month! Now let's understand that there's a chance of losing your $500 phone. But let's get real. It's your phone, TV or Toaster. You're an adult. Worst case, you will have to fork over another $500. But more than likely, you will cherish that phone, protect it, and won't lose it. You can save $120 a year. What you should do at the end of every month is look around and say, "My phone is still here and it works! My TV is still on the wall! It still works! Hey, I just found money!" Make a few purchases for electronics and don't buy the insurance, and you can save $250 or more each year. If you put the $5000 in a saving account and earned the top return, which is now 2%, you would have earned a big $100.00 for the entire year. You have already doubled that return! And you did that because you accepted the risk, you have self-insured an amount you could afford, simply because you have the $5000. That's why I don't worry about the rate of return on the $5000.

Let's not stop here. Now that you have the E Fund, you can start saving for an automobile. Not before! The great thing is that you keep saving because you're in the habit of saving. Now, let's imagine you have saved enough money, you bought the car, and now you are shopping for auto insurance. According to a survey, on average, here's what consumers across the U.S. can **save** by raising their car insurance **deductibles:** 7% if they **increase their deductible** from

$250 to $500. They could save 9% if they **raise their deductible** from $500 to $1,000. And they could save 16% by hiking **their deductible** from $500 to $2,000. With the average auto policy in California being $2000 annually, saving 16% equals $320 each year! You can do it because you have a $5000 E Fund. The list goes on and on, but stopping right here, with a saving of $320 and $250— that's $570 return on your $5000, or 11.4% annual return on your $5000 just by keeping it close to the chest in cash. Yes, you are right, you have to drive safely, and you have to protect your property. But I ask, after the prison or jail experience, are you really thinking about high speed, high-risk driving? There will be other risks. The important thing is to go through the evaluation process. Examine each risk. Ask yourself if can you avoid it? Then you don't have to do it. If you cannot avoid the risk, the next question is if you can afford to accept the risk with your E Fund $5000. You can accept a certain amount of risk. Can you reduce the risk? Think seat belts. Can you transfer the risk to another party? Can *you* insure it? This area of risk management is critical to success. How many of us know someone who was doing very well financially, and then the fortune turned on a dime because of some unfortunate event? Starting with a small step, "The E Self Insurance Fund." It will get you into the habit of saving.

If you haven't done it already, stop right now add an "E Fund" into your plan. Use the Who, What,

Where, When, Why, How and How Much formula and write out your statement. Don't forget to prioritize!. This is a *B* for important. It's not an emergency. Having this fund avoids having emergencies.

Income Target $24 Per Hour

Looking back at Quadrant II, you should have written down the income amount planned for the first 6 months, your first X. You should always be looking to make the most money for your time, but you may have to settle for a minimum wage type of job. Don't sweat it. It's fine as long as you don't plan on making it a career, and you have plans in place towards improving income. The goal is $24/hour. Here's an example of what your expenses could look like at month 7-18.

<u>Expenses:</u>
Food (includes EBT) √	$300
Rent (if necessary) √	$500
Laundry at Laundromat √	$ 40
Transportation √	$200
Walking, Bus, Car Rental, Lyft, Uber	
Auto Payment (if affordable) √	
Auto Insurance (if affordable) √	
Auto Gas (if affordable) √	
Auto Maintenance (if affordable) √	
Cell Phone √	$100

Personal Care (Haircut) √	$ 20
Medical	Out of pocket
Entertainment	
(Netflix, Easy Dining, Movie, Internet)	$200
Clothing (increase your wardrobe) √	$200
Home Improvement (if affordable) √	
Vacation	
Gifts	
Charity √*	Small Donations or Volunteer Work

If you have taken the low-end job, your monthly income, based upon $12/hour, would equal $1920 monthly. This gives you a savings rate between $360 to $960 per month, depending upon if you get the opportunity to live with friends or family, or on your own at this time. That will bring your savings total by month 18 to approximately $6480 to $17,280. Keep in mind that your target income should still be $24/hour or around $4000 per month. The $6480 is kind of a minimum but very realistic. The real challenge in months 7-18 isn't really in the income. It's doing your best to maintain minimal expenses. Once you get some money in your pocket, the urge to spend arrives.

I have a suggestion here, start thinking of what you can do legally to earn $24/hour. You may need to go to school; you may have to get a license. Start making that list: Uber, Lyft, and others. Amazon, as of this writing, is paying $15/hour, which is great but still doesn't work. Your target is $24/hour or more.

Start incorporating it into your plan. It's not unrealistic and very achievable when you own a business.

Think of starting a business even while working at the low paying job. It takes a lot of work. You may be working 7 days a week. But it's worth it. Write that into your plan: "**At Months 7-18,** I plan on doing XYZ." But add the following lines: "Staying as strong as I can to continue to keep my expenses to the absolute minimum and save as much money as possible."

Need More Help?

Do you remember the song by the Killers, "Mr. Brightside"? "Coming out of my cage and I doin' just fine, fine." Well, in the first six months, just after getting out of the cage, you're so happy to be free again. It's way beyond really "doing just fine, fine"—it's fantastic. But there's a lot of temptation when you start to accumulate money. You've lived on 15¢ Ramen Soup, Bologna, and Peanut Butter for a very long time. Let's face it, if you're starting with nothing, you're a long way from building a life. So I am going to summarize the following expenses verbally and hope that it helps you in developing your plan. This should prepare you for phase two. After you read this narrative, using the $24/hour target, write out your planning statement for months 7-18. Use Who, What, Where, When, Why, How, and How Much. Don't forget to add in Quadrant II B2 Target an income of $24/hour.

Month 7-18 Narrative

Your target Rent/Mortgage expense is suggested to be $2000/month. But, unless you have an existing home to come back home to, that's not realistic. Still, consider keeping it as your target because it will be affordable down the road.

To eat really healthy, we have targeted $300/month during this time. Food Stamps will get you by initially and should still be available to you for at least part of the 7-18th month period. Once your income level rises, you can start spending a little more, putting significant energy into maintaining healthy eating habits.

The cell phone is an essential item. If you do have the money, by all means, get the best that money can buy. For all the reasons we have already discussed, we have an expense targeted range of $100/month. It may get slightly higher but not much more. If you don't have the money, no worries, stick with your LifeLine Phone for now since it's free for the first 12 months. Then they reevaluate your need. The same with the Food Stamp program.

If you have a car and the money, by all means, use it. But if you don't have the money, hold off and walk and use public transportation. Believe me, you can make it work. It's $200/month! You can rent a car when you really need it. Save your money. There is no need to spend precious cash at this time on gasoline, insurance, registration fees, and automobile maintenance.

Use $20/month and go get yourself a proper hair cut. Yes, it's going to cost more than a banana or two soups, but it's worth it. As you plan to start your new business or look for a new job, remember that you "never get a second chance to make a first impression." For right now, $40/month for laundry is more than enough.

Medical Expenses will eventually cost at minimum $100/month, but for now, while on Parole/Probation, let the State/County do its job while you are still under supervision.

Plan for $200/month for entertainment. This should cover things like going to a movie, going out to dinner, bowling, or paying for streaming services. In the first six months, you relied upon friends and family for your entertainment. Now, at month 7, you've done a great job and can consider spending the $200.

You will need to build your wardrobe. It's suggested to do so at the rate of $200/month, but again use the strategy mentioned at the Salvation Army Family Store. Now expand your wardrobe at Costco and Walmart.

Try and hold off as long as possible before you start thinking about spending $200/month for home improvements. This is not construction or home repairs. This is referring to buying a set of plates and silverware, a TV, a toaster, towels, cleaning fluids, scented candles, blankets, a bed, lamps, etc. It is suggested that you do not make major purchases without having the money in hand first. So you are putting aside $200/month. Each month you can gradually rebuild your household needs. You've had nothing for so long, so have patience in the comeback process. Be thankful to God every step of the way.

Stop now and think about this. Write out your plan using Who, What, Where, When, Why, How and How Much.

Months 7-18 Some More Helpful Thoughts

A Place to Live: Again, you're writing your own plan. The numbers will be different for everyone. So just consider what I'm sharing, thinking it through out loud. Do not be discouraged if you don't meet your expectations, this is not an exact science. Go back and make adjustments. If you were able to get a job immediately following your release, "Park the Money!" Try to live within the guidelines above. At the seventh month marker, start thinking, "it's time to improve." The Seventh Month Marker? As the first item on the list, you can start looking for a place to live, not a month to month. Try at least for a year. This will give you some stability— a place to put your stuff and transition away from the family or friend you may have been living with.

The price range for a rental room is around $500-800 per month. Be cautious as to whom you may be living with. Remember, you're still on probation, and you don't need any drama or law enforcement issues. Try and get a lease in hand for a year. If you can, try to find a location near work. You will be way ahead of the game. Safe, nice, and no drama. Take your time and find the right place. You can afford it even if you have a minimum wage job. Remember, your target expense for a place to live longterm is $2000/month. If you do a good job in this area by hitting your income targets by the time you reach your 36th month out of custody, you should be able to afford your own home! One step at a time, but create your place to live statement in your plan at the 7-18th month mark and remember: Who, What, Where, When, Why, How, and How Much.

Food: You have done a good job and stretched the food stamp dollars to the max with little or no out of pocket. You're working now. The target for this time period is $300/month. Your 36 month mark target is $500/month, which includes fast-food restaurants, groceries, and health and beauty aids. But we are not there yet. I suggest that you modestly increase this budget and enjoy a greater variety of healthy food. Enjoy, on occasion, a few fast-food restaurants. Don't hold on to the food stamps as long as they will allow.

Once you are in a position to buy quality food with your own money, call them and tell them you don't need it anymore. It is the right thing to do. Let the next person in line use it. Regardless of if you do or don't, one day you will be paying for all of your own food. This is part of the process of joining the real world and getting off the social services programs and start independently living life. Write it out: Who, What, Where, When, Why, How, and How Much.

Cellphone: This is a big one. For many reasons, this is the place to splurge. Today the cellphone has become a gateway to connect, build, manage, and maintain your relationships. Beyond that, it is a gateway that opens to a new world and a new level of productivity and cost-saving. There is literally a phone application for everything. If they haven't invented it, you may want to be the one to do so— and make a fortune in the process. You need a ride? There are Uber and Lyft, just to name a few. Need to check your bank balance? There's an app for that. Want to check to see the balance on your credit card or credit score? Just look at your phone. If you need directions, with an iPhone, all you have to say is, "Hey Siri, Navigate Me to Wherever." If you are cooking and need to set a timer, simply say, "Hey Siri, Set An Alarm For 20 minutes." If you need a reminder to see your Parole Officer, say, "Hey Siri, Set A Reminder." This is a very, very valuable tool and can be used for almost every aspect of your life: personal, family, friends, spiritual, and business. So it's highly recommended that you plan on purchasing the best, newest, and most sophisticated iPhone possible. Your LifeLine phone has served its purpose. Now that you have the money, it's time to move on and improve. This is a very sophisticated tool— portable and quick. The internet is always attached and easy to use. Buy the best, learn everything about it, and use this tool to help you improve your daily life and achieve your goals. The estimated monthly expense of $100/month is more than enough for a single user with unlimited everything. Now that you heard all the good stuff on how this tool can change your life for the better, we need to talk about how an iPhone can also ruin your life. How? Along with all those great productive features, there are also a lot of entertainment features. The worst part of it is that it's way too easy to buy things online with your phone. Yes, Darth Vader is right there, bombarding you again with texts and advertisements from the moment you wake up. Even worse, with a few pushes, taps, or a swipe, your product is on its way— sometimes in less than 4 hours! This is a budget killer. So get ready, Luke. You need to use the force and stay strong whenever the Dark Side starts to takes hold. Instead of swiping and tapping your way to bankruptcy, wait a day and ask yourself: "Self, do you really need this now?" Even with this big downside, the iPhone is a way too valuable tool not to have. So **go for it!** Start researching at the 6-month marker, whether you have a great job or not, this is a must upgrade. Put in on your list in Quadrant I: Who, What, Where, When, Why, How, and How Much

Transportation: As crazy as I am about the cell phones, I'm not very excited at all about automobiles, even at the 7-month marker. It is much better to wait and reevaluate at the 18-month mark. The only exception would be if you have already accumulated your E Fund at the 6-month marker and have a good job, paying at least $24/hour. At that point, it's open for consideration.

Patience is key here. You are in recovery. Like most of us, you are starting over from scratch, and the worst thing you can do for yourself is to try and rush this process. It took a while to get into this mess in the first place. So how do you deal with impatience and worry about the unknowns to be? Faith, put your trust in God. He is there for you. Pray, pray, and pray again. You are not alone. He is watching over everything. Prayer makes you stand out from the rest. Pray with emotion, and God will forgive you. Pray with an attentive heart and see all of Heaven's doors open before you. Pray with joy, and watch your requests ascend straight to God's chamber. Pray for patience, be grateful, and thank God every day for every accomplishment— big or small. You are not alone. Do it! Write it out: Who, What, Where, When, Why, How, and How Much

Planning For Months 19-36 and Beyond

Freedom! Eighteen months have passed now. Some of you are off parole or probation. You have been earning money, and now it's time to **stop**! Look what you have just done! Now is the time to reflect on your accomplishments and praise God and be thankful for everything. Think of it like taking a helicopter ride away, up from where you are standing, and look down at what you achieved. If you stayed focused through the transition wholeheartedly, you should have 18 months of sobriety, surrounded by supportive people. It's like an internal light shining, letting you know where you are going— with family and friends who believe in you. It's not just good, it's heroic! You have been blessed by the Lord because you're walking in God's way. Let me suggest that you talk to God each night in your owns words as you would a friend. Share with Him what you want to accomplish, thank Him for all that He has done, and continue to focus and build your trust in Him. Even with all your hard work, it will be God who will be the one to make it happen. Never believe anything else. If something has not happened that you really want or wish to happen, focus every ounce of your concentration on that thing or event. Visualize it in fine detail. If your desire is strong enough and concentration intense enough, pray, and you can make it come true. Remember, money is just a tool, just one part of a balanced life. Money-worship, like idol-worship, stems from a lack of trust in God. The more it is uprooted, the more the world radiates with the blessing of the Holy One's Love.

Your focus for the next 19 months and beyond is accumulation, with a disciplined approach to savings. You should not be thinking of investing. Keep accumulating for your first major purchase, which should be a home. By purchasing a home, you will be able to convert the rent you are now paying. The *expense* becomes an *asset* using the wise use of *leverage*. As we will discuss in Chapter 9, I will illustrate several strategies to acquire a home for little or no money down. Keep saving your money! Write out your home purchase goals into your plan: What, Where, When, Why, How, and How Much method. Write in your 18-month income goal of $4000/month. At month 19, you should be out of custody, and even if you're not, you will have the ability to move. If you are thinking about moving, I have listed a variety of locations to think about towards the end of the book.

Monthly Income Target : $4128
(which is $24 X 40 Hours X 4.3 weeks in a month)

Monthly Expenses:

Expense	Earning Years	During Custody
Rent/Mortgage	$2000	$0
Food	$500	$0
Cellphone	$100	$0
Transportation	$300	$0
Insurance	$100	$0
Personal Care	$20	$0
Laundry	$25	$0
Medical	$100	$0
Entertainment	$200	$0
Clothing	$200	$0
Home Expenses	$200	$0
Vacation	$100	$0
Gifts	$100	$0
Charity	$100	$0

By now you should have a pretty good idea of the future. You have possibly awakened in the middle of the night with your head spinning with ideas. That is all part of the process. Again, it's really a good idea to keep a note pad by your bed or under your pillow to jot down whatever comes to mind in the middle of the night. I recommend this for two reasons. One, it will help you sleep better because you won't have to deal with the anxiety of worrying about what you're going to forget by the time you wake back up in the morning. Secondly, those ideas in the middle of the night are usually fantastic ideas.

Remember, this is your personal plan, and it does not involve those who are living next to you, above you, below you, or with whom you socialize in the yard. Also, leave plenty of space between your sentences so you can easily make changes. Write in pencil if you can. Obviously, those who are in jail or prison reception have no choice. But writing your plan in pencil is a good thing here. It will make it easier for you to make changes. With a plan in hand, you're ready to move on.

Months 19-36 Narrative

You now have been working for 18 months. For many of you, you are off of parole and probation. If you are very comfortable with the place you are, by all means, keep on saving for as long as you can. You should be way beyond your E Fund. You could start looking at other places to live. Keep in mind the strategies that I have included in the chapters to follow on how to acquire a home for little or no money down. If you haven't purchased a vehicle, please don't do it on my account, but only if you need one. You could look for a vehicle within the parameters set in the cash flow listed above. Do your best to beat the numbers if you can. But certainly, don't exceed the numbers. The financial engine has just started here. Patience. This is a three-year plan.

Groceries are now at the $500/month expense mark. Whatever you can do to save, **without** it affecting healthy eating, by all means, do it. It's all additional savings. Saving will get you to your financial goals sooner. You should now have a high powered iPhone, which we have covered.

Medical Insurance, hopefully, is covered by your employer. If you are working for yourself, it's time to step up and pay the piper. You need good coverage, but you also can carry a high deductible to save money. Remember, we are trying to self-insure the things we can afford because we have an E-Fund. We transfer the risk to an insurance company for the things we cannot afford to lose, such as losing your job because of a major disability or from a major illness.

A target of $200/month for entertainment is more than enough. If you don't use it, add it to savings. That goes for the clothing and home expenses, as well.

Vacation is important. You have come a long way, and you need to take a break. $100/month is $1200 a year. Vegas and Cruises are half that. It's also time to give small gifts to those you love and those who have helped you thus far. You need to go the extra mile and help those less fortunate than you. Give back through charity. Personally, I give money directly to the homeless. I also support both the LA Mission and other non-profits. You've been blessed, it's time to help others. There's also an application on your phone that will help. Amazing tool, the iPhone.

Try to have your plan completely written at this point before moving on. Leave plenty of space to add stuff or cross out. Now, I am moving on to Pre-Release and Release, most of which is all a narrative of my experience. Once you read it, you are going to want to add more items to your list. Just remember, what you have written does not have to be perfect or the final list. After you have finished the book, you can go back and re-write the plan. Then begin the process of getting things done and checking them off daily. What an amazing feeling it is— trust me on that. Anything you can get done, even the smallest things, while in custody, is a total blessing.

CHAPTER 6

Pre-Release Plan Implementation

Around the 90th to 120th day, near your Earliest Possible Release Date (EPRD), the California State Prison System computer alarm kicks in. Your Correctional Counselor Records Analyst (or CCRA) is given the task of reviewing your file in detail. They then begin calculating what is needed to process, collect, and put together the paperwork and documentation necessary for your release. Up to this point, the CCRA is supposed to look at your file regularly. Most of the time they look to see if there are any additional charges to add on, write-ups, and other disciplinary activity. So usually, they are looking to add more time to your sentence. There are always exceptions, but in general, they really don't study your file in detail to try to reduce your sentence.

That means the last time someone really looked at your case file in detail was when you were first transferred to a mainline prison from your prison reception center.

Do not, and let me repeat, do not wait for the 90-120th day. Start preparing for your release the moment you get there—even if it's 2 years away. If you are in a California State Prison, immediately make sure to order a current copy of your Legal Status Summary. Make sure you know what every number and every code represents. If you do not understand it, request clarification, and if it doesn't make sense, ask again.

The Court System and The California Department of Corrections and Rehabilitation are notorious for making huge sentencing errors and think nothing of it. We had inmates who were given wrong release dates, some early and some late. Can you imagine the feeling of being told you're being released on a particular date, only to find out a day or two before leaving, that you have another two months or two years to serve?! It happened 6 times while I was in Fire Camp. One inmate who lived across from me had paperwork saying that he was leaving in December. The family was excited since he had been away for two years. The family made a reservation in Las Vegas. They were planning to celebrate. Then they found out that the powers that be made a mistake, and now the date is in January. Or how about this... One of the lead cooks in our kitchen is 90 days out. The prison did an audit on his sentencing only to find out that his sentence was incorrectly calculated. He should have been released 2 years earlier, and they had to order an emergency release! Yes, this is real, and it happens all the time. It's nuts! Do not become brain lazy. You want to get out and stay out.

Let's also not forget you may have to deal with holds from ICE (Immigration and Customs Enforcement). You need to find out if you have any outstanding warrants and previous parole holds. They, too, will need to be resolved. Start the process as early as possible by using an inmate request Form C22 and secure a copy of your legal status summary. Get used to using the forms. Make sure that you understand it, and the information is correct. Do not believe for a minute that if it's wrong in your favor, you are going to get away with it. It's not going to happen. Let's say you were sentenced for three years, but that you have your earliest possible release date a year from now. At 120 days before your date, they will do the audit and give you the bad news whenever they feel like it. That could be months, weeks, or a day before your supposed release. It happens every day. So get it squared away and save yourself the disapoints.

Oh, and by the way, while in Wasco, an inmate was released two weeks early by mistake. He got released and went home to his wife and family. The next day the police arrived at his house. Do they give him an ankle bracelet, or make some house arrest arrangements? No, they put the handcuffs on and just brought him back to the same dorm, until the two weeks are over. It's crazy!

At this point, you now know the importance of establishing and nurturing relationships before your release. While in jail, I had the honor of hearing a lot of stories on how people found themselves in jail. One pattern repeated itself so many times that it's worth mentioning, especially if it applies to you or someone you know. It was common to see young men 18,19, and 20 years old, unmarried with young children. They are in custody for drug sales or a crime committed trying to support their young family. The mother and children are now living with her parents. She is working full-time at a job she had to take, and the grandparents are raising the children. The grandparents also think that the father of their grandchildren is the lowest form of slime on the planet. After all, he got himself in trouble, abandoned their baby daughter and their grandchildren, and put all the responsibility on them. A lot is going on here. This book in no way sums up all the issues. Still, I can tell you this from experience: Spending 5 months in jail in a barracks setting, I had the opportunity to counsel many with this exact circumstance. I offered some guidance with great success. If you fit into this category, let me take a moment to share part of what was discussed. I recommend that if you love the mother of your children, show your intentions to your future wife and her parents and make plans to marry (while in custody). Get some money on the phone, and secondly, start a humbling dialogue with her parents. Let them know you screwed up, you are sorry, and you will make it up to them. The parents should be included in your financial plan (under Family and Friends). Let them know you intend to help them financially when you are back on your feet.

Although no one can predict how things might turn out, in one case I was able to get some honest feedback. I found out that the young man did, in fact, marry the mother of his children, ended up living with the in-laws, and worked for his father-in-law's company.

The lesson to be learned here is to take the time and put lots of effort into rebuilding your relationships with your family, friends, and God. *This is Priceless.* So go back, if necessary, and add it to your financial plan: What, Where, When, Why, How, and How Much.

Another very important thing to do is to get yourself in a mental state of Joy. Always remember: Joy is not just merely incidental; it is your spiritual quest. It is vital. Nothing is as liberating as joy. It frees the mind and fills it with tranquility. You need to be in good mental spirits to write a new life plan.

Stop worrying! Losing hope is like losing your freedom, like losing yourself. Don't listen to the guards. They are just paid employees whose best interests are served by keeping you in custody as long as possible. They also justify their mistreatment of you under a false veil of rehabilitation. They are not psychologists, they are guards. So don't support their cause. Don't give them one extra minute of satisfaction with your life. And don't get caught up in the prison or jail bullshit.

On the other hand, research all your exit options like Medi-Cal, Social Security, getting a State ID, arranging a place to live, and arranging release transportation. Do your best to try not to take the bus or the train home. See if you can get someone to pick you up. If you can arrange your healthcare, do it. If you can arrange employment, do it, too.

Don't be discouraged if you can't get all this stuff done. The system is not on your side. They work against you. This is not easy stuff, and they don't make it easy for you. Anything and everything is ridiculously hard to do.

In Jamestown, you had to place your prison identification card, on certain days, into a plastic bag. Then an inmate and a guard would shake up the bag and pull out a hand full of cards. Then they would call them out. If you were lucky and your card was called, you were given a time and a phone to use. If the sirens go off on the yard, that's it. Stop what you are doing, get on the ground, your telephone call is lost. Odd number dorms could call on certain days (and even on others). And that's just to make a phone call, assuming someone put some money on the phone and was willing to talk to you. You had to stand outside and wait all day for an open line spot to speak to a counselor. You wait weeks for responses on those C22 forms. Even the mail service was ultra slow. Don't be discouraged. Celebrate every night before you fall off to sleep. Celebrate every little accomplishment along the way. The more you can accomplish before your release, the less you will have to deal with after and the better you will feel.

CHAPTER 7

Post Release & Plan Implementation

Mental preparation: No matter how far you've strayed, returning to God is always possible. Agree, therefore, that there is absolutely no place for despair. Never despair! Never! It is forbidden for you to give up hope. "Cast **your burden** upon **God**, and He will sustain you." (Psalms 55:23) and remember that things can go from the very worst to the very best in just a blink of an eye.

Sensitivity, Change, and Transformation: You need to develop sensitivity to what has just happened to you. It doesn't matter what you have done in the past, what you have been taught, or habits that you have created. Those were the things that brought you to the point of incarceration.

You need to reach deep inside and become sensitive to those feelings. They can be feelings of fear, vulnerability, rejection, hunger, or anger. That's a shortlist. There's a very long list of potential feelings. You need to become sensitive to all of them. Once you become sensitive to these feelings, you want to learn to sense it coming. Take a step back, pause to that realization, and think about it before taking action. You may have to sleep on it or discuss it with a trusted friend or pray to God for a solution. Regardless, you do not want to fall back into the same pattern of reacting to your emotions as before.

It's not only feelings, but it's also actions as well. Once you have developed that sensitivity to those feelings and actions of the past, you can start considering other options that will change your course. Here's an example of actions and feelings in real life:

You have always been in credit card debt. Your parents were always in debt, and all of your friends were always in debt. Every month almost everything you earned was spent on the basics and credit card payments. When you had a little bit extra, it burned in your pocket (the feeling). This was so out of control that you had to get rid of the money. You would buy something mindlessly, simply because you were not used to having any deposable income in your pocket.

Now that you are sensitive to this feeling, you can start to change the course. But remember, it's going to take will power to keep money in your pocket. You may have to avoid looking at advertisements. You may have to cancel subscriptions— become an "unsubscribe maniac" with all of the email advertisements. You may have to start studying about saving money to occupy your free time. Hang around with other people who are frugal with their finances.

If you become sensitive to these forces, you can learn to respect the forces that are out there doing their best to separate you from your money. You will start to make changes in your lifestyle. It changes the way you think about the "must-haves." The transformation begins, and you start with the ability to accumulate money with a feeling of satisfaction, not spending anything. It's a new level of inner happiness. You are no longer going to be broke, and you're going to have a very bright financial future ahead of you.

Finding your place to live: Hopefully, you've mended a few relations and have found a tranquil place to transition. Reading this workbook, you now know the value of mending those damaged relationships from your prior acts and incarceration. Hopefully, the mending resulted in you having at least a temporary place to stay upon your release.

If, for some reason, on the day of your release, you're left alone on the street, and you're not participating in a program established by probation or parole, head to a Mission.

There are many Missions. I've listed only The Union Rescue Mission in Los Angeles, founded in 1891. They have a very comprehensive program that includes a place to sleep, along with health care with dental, legal aid, education, maintenance, and support. There are Missions in almost every county and large cities. Missions can help provide the basics you need to move forward.

Also, finally, politicians are becoming more active, especially in California, which has possibly the largest homeless population in the world. By the time you read this book, hopefully, even more programs will emerge. The bottom line is that you need to do whatever you can to be off the street when you are released.

We had around 80 men in custody in a barracks setting in the Orange County Jail at the Theo Lacy Facility. Some went to court and were released that night. I asked them, "Where are you going?" and "Who's picking you up?" Without a penny in their pocket at 12:01, they were leaving that jail with no place to go.

I'm told that it takes around 3 to 4 hours before you start getting hungry. You want to be prepared. I had the potential opportunity to be released into an Alternate Custody Program. These folks at the Union Rescue Mission offered to help in any way they could. When I was offered this place as a potential way of getting out of prison, my son Robert and his family got in the car and drove from Orange County all the way down to downtown Los Angeles to visit the Mission. My son said, "Dad, this is skid row. People are living on the street everywhere. But inside the Mission, it's clean and comfortable. Everyone I met was there to get you back on your feet." They asked for nothing in return and said money is not needed; they are well funded by donations.

The Union Rescue Mission
545 S San Pedro St
Los Angeles, California 90013
(213) 347-6300

Here's the Mission Statement from the Union Rescue Mission.
The Guiding Principles:

- We serve God, under the Lordship of Jesus Christ and:
- We will serve the whole person in mind, body, and spirit
- We will always serve others with humility
- We will treat all people, who are created in the image of God, with dignity and respect
- We will meet, or exceed, the expectations of those we serve
- We will actively find new ways to be good stewards of the resources entrusted to us

- We will be truthful and accountable in our work together
- We will do what we say we will do
- We will intentionally look at new and innovative ways to do our work
- We will share our expertise with others

Think about that. They practice what they preach!

On Another Note, Here's Some New Information: At a hearing on Monday, October 29th, 2018, Judge David O. Carter said to residents of Orange County, officials, and supporters of the homeless that he has toured the Santa Ana River homeless encampment site twice. He said that efforts are being made to help the street populations in the area represent "a journey no other county has taken."

The City of Costa Mesa will sign on soon to a 12-bed crisis center and a 50 bed-facility expected to open by next summer. The City of Tustin is planning for a 50-bed shelter run by the Orange County Rescue Mission. The City of Anaheim is partnering with the Salvation Army to launch a 200-bed operation. It also has another 125-bed project planned on private property owned by businessman Bill Taormina.

"This means that more of the homeless will be inside at the start of the rainy season," said Brooke Weitzman, an attorney representing seven homeless adults against the county and several cities, who sought to prevent their evictions from the illegal encampment. "We are so glad to see that these cities are showing goodwill, and especially that Santa Ana has cut through the red tape to assemble a team to take quick action."

The legal settlement between advocates for the homeless and officials from Orange County stalled at the hearing Monday, while many cities in south Orange County have refused to offer temporary housing.

Lawyers for the homeless and the county unveiled a draft agreement last week that committed to shelter options suited for a range of homeless needs, including those who are victims of domestic abuse and violence.

Areas of ongoing negotiation include:
1. Developing procedures to guarantee due process for the indigent.
2. Figuring out how to store property seized from individuals and couples.
3. Creating guidelines to respond to those seeking accommodation under the Americans with Disabilities Act.

In a separate lawsuit filed in February 2019, the Legal Aid Society of Orange County, working on behalf of the People's Homeless Task Force and seven disabled adults who lived at the riverbed, maintained that evictions are discriminatory and that officials didn't have adequate services in place for their clients with special needs.

Plaintiffs, in both cases, accused officials of trying to criminalize homelessness. At the hearing Monday, cities in the southern part of the county came under attack for their inaction.

"I will not support a settlement without all cities named in the lawsuit," said Andrew Do, chairman of the Orange County Board of Supervisors. "North and central Orange County are building homeless shelter space, while south county is rewarded for fear-mongering and obstruction... Santa Ana, Orange, Costa Mesa, and Anaheim cannot continue to bear the full burden of this countywide crisis."

With respect to all parties involved, it is your job to use this opportunity only if you have to and only for a transitional period of time. It is your responsibility to become independent and living a clean, honest life on your own. It is just not that hard to do. Like I told all my children, "You work hard, good things happen." It really is that simple.

At certain points in life, you just cannot stall things. Decisions that seem tough, painful, and even unjust have to be made for the sake of your own well-being. Survival instincts will often dictate that you stall things and live in the sun for a while longer. But biting the bullet and making important decisions at crucial times will make life a bit brighter in general, even though you won't see it right then and there.

The worst thing you can do is to refuse to accept your mistakes. One of the many ways to undo that is by being decisive. If you could just stop and perceive your thoughts, you would see that you give yourself excuses all the time! There is not one thing right now that you can't do. And if you look at it firmly that way, you only lack decisiveness and dedication. Don't let your mind play games with you. The only thing your mind wants is to be safe. Feeling uncomfortable is the key to success in everything you do. So try to get out of your comfort zone.

You Are Not Behind Bars Anymore.
Let's Expand on what has already been discussed.

Transportation. One of the most significant expenses in the early stages of your release is an automobile. If you're starting over from scratch at this point, now is just not the time to be thinking about cars. This is not the time to be making payments on cars, repairs, insurance, etc. You do not want to be susceptible to incarceration because of an accident or having the wrong person in the car or a substance—or both. I realize that everywhere you go, it seems like every television ad and internet ad is an automobile ad. With the amount the auto industry spends on advertising, it's tough to resist. But as of this writing, a record 7 million Americans are 90 days behind on their auto payments! Stay away from cars for now. Don't let your ego get to you, especially for the first six months. Just stay out of the car. What I do recommend, as I discussed earlier, is to use public transportation for your daily commute to work or even better, just walk or both. They have all kinds of special programs for the bus, for me, being 66 years old, I paid $1.50 for unlimited use of the bus every day. I also walk half the time. It is really helpful to combine a bunch of things together that require a car, like an out of the area medical appointment or running around town shopping or buying water at the market. Water tends to be a bit heavy to carry around with you. So what do you do? When you can afford it, you rent an inexpensive car for a day or two. I needed to do my taxes, go shopping in three locations (Walmart, Target, and the 99¢ Store), go to the Salvation Army. I added a Taco Bell run for lunch. Then I returned the vehicle in the morning. $40. When you're on your feet again, you can consider buying a car. But initially keep it lean and mean. There are always Uber and Lyft in case of short trip emergencies. If a family member or close friend has a car, remember to use it only when you have to. Do not spend money on gasoline right now.

Things To Think About If You Are Living with a Friend or Family Member

Don't get too comfortable. You're blessed by having family and friends helping you out with a place to stay, but it should be considered just a stepping stone. Once you have obtained employment and have all your public assistance in place, you will eventually be looking for your own living arrangements. Take care of the DMV, professional licenses, church visit, food stamps, Cal Fresh, Cal Works, general relief, LifeLine phone, medical clinics, Social Security, retirement, or Disability. Please remember to be well organized when dealing with these government agencies. Make sure to keep a record of your passwords and websites. Take your transition seriously. Stay focused!

Being in custody slows your mind down. What could have been, should have been, might have been... if you did it right but didn't. Time travel is still a theory. Just accept the fact that in life, things often fall apart. Most good things, no matter how strong they seem at first, can and will fall apart. Brooding over the possibilities of what could have been and should have been is not something wise to do. If you can't change it, why think about it? Think about it as a part of life and a growing experience. But convince your mind that it is in the past. Regret will eat you up alive. It could only be present if YOU are actually not present. Stay in the NOW. This is the only place things are happening. Time to move forward.

Sober Living Programs. Sober living programs come in many sizes and shapes, but for our purposes, there are only a few programs paid for by the state and programs paid for by the county. Most of these programs follow the same pattern. For the first three months or more, you are, for the most part, locked up in a home with no unsupervised outside access or contact. You participate in expanded Celebrate Recovery-type program. Gradually, you are permitted freedoms with curfews. Then you are expected to do your daily life functions, find work, and eventually become independent. The feedback from many of these places is that drugs are being used, and there is poor supervision. This is probably because they are at no cost to the inmate, and maybe there isn't enough motivation. The supervisors are supposed to be drug testing almost daily. Probation and parole officers are supposed to be making regular visits and searches. But from what I'm told, it's not the best place to be if you are trying to stay sober.

One of my friends who was released into one of these homes had an experience where 3 cop cars showed up at 10 p.m. They were looking for a parolee. They came to the front door and asked for the person. As soon as they saw him, they walked into the house and put him in handcuffs while they searched his room and his car. They found drugs in the car. That's a parole violation, and off to jail he went.

You want no drama. You want out of this. You want a peaceful place to get your life in order. It seems like sober living programs run by the county and state are just not the right ticket. From what I was told about these sober living programs, they are nothing short of party time with other addicts— daily life of frequent visits from the police, arrests, and neighborhood complaints. The neighborhood is in an uproar because of all the drug dealing and all-nighters. That's why it's so important to build relationships with friends and family who can change your social environment.

Sober Living Homes. This is not as good as living with family and friends, but a much better choice than a program, if you can get into one. Most of these Sober Living Homes are owned by private individuals who are landlords, not a manager or supervisors. In a Sober Living Home, from day one, you're living the life of a free man. You are renting a room, either private or shared. But the owners of these homes, in order to maintain their business status as a sober living home, need to keep you sober. That's their business. Most of them are situated in really nice residential areas, and they want no drama or complaints from the neighbors. They can drug test you as part of the rental agreement. I was once considering going to one of these homes because I was having a hard time finding a room. I was able to talk to the owner on a one-on-one, who told me he runs a clean home. If any resident is found drinking or using drugs, they are asked to leave immediately.

On the other hand, there are not many restrictions other than you paying rent. To maintain your residency, sometimes you may have to participate in a stepped recovery program or you may also be tested regularly for drug or alcohol use. Thinking out loud, in reality, all of these programs are not very much help. You are living with people who have the very lifestyle you need to change to be successful.

If you have serious drug issues, you need a serious long-term drug rehabilitation program.

Room Rental. Because of the shortage of affordable housing in many areas of the country, Room Rentals have become popular. You sacrifice a little privacy, but the accommodations and price make it a great place to start getting back on your feet. Plus, technology has brought numerous phone applications and websites to match renter and landlord. Even if you don't have a strong credit report or above-average income, the value it gives you is the ability to save money. That's a primary goal, especially during the critical first 6-12 month period.

If you go this route, I suggest that you try and find a place with very little to no drama. Remember, your parole/probation officer will be visiting and can and will conduct a search of your room. I personally found success in this area using CraigsList. The landlords were very straight forward with their wants. For example: Single Adult Male, Must Have Full-Time Employment, No Pets, No Smoking, etc. So you get dressed, show up, and have a one-on-one. Be sure to meet anyone who lives there to get a good feel for the place. **DO NOT, I REPEAT, DO NOT SHARE YOUR CRIMINAL HISTORY!** Here are some good questions to ask:

- ☐ Are utilities included?
- ☐ How many people live in this house?

- How long have they lived there? Long-term renters show you that there is stability here and a responsible landlord, most of the time.
- Can you have a sleepover guest?

If you are there in the summer, notice if the air conditioning is on or just the windows open. In the winter, notice if the heat on and if the house feels warm. If it feels right, it probably is right, and you should consider the location.

I suggest that you find several locations and do not buy into the fact that there is someone else on the hook, and you "have to act fast now." Forget that, this is an important decision. If you rent a room, there are a few things I suggest that you do:
- Make sure you follow all the rules of the house.
- Make sure to clean up after yourself.
- Be courteous and understanding with regards to the bathroom and kitchen.
- Do a few things that are not in the contract, like take out the kitchen garbage or wash someone else dishes. You could buy toilet paper, paper towels, or bathroom spray.
- You want to be considered a perfect tenant to everyone.

Remember, your life can be instantly complicated by a visit from the parole/probation officers who could walk in with Black Flack Jackets that say **County Probation Department** with guns at their sides. On the other hand, they could be the supportive type and wear T-shirts and shorts, and you can call them your cousin.

The other factor you need to be aware of is that the County Sheriff has a list of everyone in their county on Parole/Probation, and nothing stops them from driving up to the house and knocking on the door. They could ask anyone who answers if you are there. Then they would request your presence, walk in, and put you in handcuffs while another officer goes into your room and does a detailed search. When that happens, you will probably have to come clean, that you have been released from prison or jail, and now it's all good. You want to be in good favor with everyone you live with and not have deal with "**We are not comfortable with you living here**" and "**Please find another place to live.**"

It makes sense, once you do get a place to live, that you would want to call your probation/parole office immediately. They don't like surprises.

Lastly, you can use this rental room as your mailing address. But if you think you are going to be moving around, go to one of those mailbox places like Goin Postal, Postal Annex, or The UPS Store. They can give you a street address with your rented box. If you are in Lake Forest, California, Goin Postal / Cast Global Shipping on Aspan Street has the lowest cost mailboxes anywhere, plus you get package delivery at no additional charge. Make sure you're within walking distance and set up a personal private mailbox. Remember, you will get mail from probation or the state, and you may want to maintain your privacy. Also remember, do not share your criminal history with a Landlord or Employer unless asked. Do share it with your Banker and your Doctors.

Apartment Rentals. For most of you, this is not an option. Getting an apartment typically will require the first and last month's rent, a good source of income, and a clean credit report. If you have those in hand and six months of fixed expenses, you are ready for an independent life. Apartment rentals here in Orange County run around $1600/month, plus utilities. In other words, $2000/month. Most landlords require a minimum commitment of a year to get that price. With a shorter rental time, you're going to pay more. With cash reserves in hand and the ability to fork out $1600 plus utilities, you are a stone's throw away from owning a home with little or no money down. The focus of this book is starting from scratch. Renting an apartment would be a consideration only sometime after the 18th month and realistically only after the 36th month. Save your money, you will need it.

Saddleback Church Bulletin Board. Yes! The Saddleback Church website has a bulletin board set up that members use to post rooms wanted and rooms available for rent.

http://bb.saddleback.com

This is a fantastic source, especially if you are connected to the Church either by participating in a Celebrate Recovery Program, volunteering, or as a member. Church members and affiliates like to live with other members and affiliates of the Church. They feel more comfortable, and you get the extra possibility of participating at the Church with your landlord or roommates. It's just all good and builds strong relationships. Saddleback has churches all over California and the World! What a great spiritual family to be involved in— a family who understands where you have been and can help you, God willing, to get where you're going.

Probation/Parole and Your Probation/Parole Officer. Regardless of whether you are released on probation or parole or some combination of the two, you will be assigned a probation officer. Your probation officer can be a blessing or your worst nightmare, depending on how you handle yourself from the get-go. Upon your release, you will be requested to check in at the main parole headquarters. This could be the day following your release, or it could be several days after your release, depending on your type of case and level of risk determined. The most important part of this is to be there. If for some reason, you cannot get there, you have to make sure you call and let them know, or you can find yourself back behind bars. It's that quick. Once at the main headquarters, if you have issues, need food or a place to stay, this is an excellent time to plead your case. After your initial meeting, you will be assigned a probation/parole officer and given a date to see that person. Again make sure you arrive ahead of schedule and show your willingness to be as accommodating and respectful as possible. Don't expect a handshake or socializing. Expect to be drug tested and asked where you are living. Be totally honest and upfront. And, for heaven's sake, don't break any rules. They will hand you a list of guidelines. Make sure you understand them all. You will be asked to sign off on them. Remember that you are still in custody until released from probation or parole.

When I was out on parole, my first stop was on Main Street in Santa Ana in sort of a lobby/police station-looking place. After waiting in the lobby, my name was called, and I was given some paperwork with instructions to meet my probation officer in Costa Mesa, California. The only trouble was that Costa Mesa was not where I was living. I was living in Lake Forest. The Costa Mesa address was given to them when I signed my parole paperwork, which was 6 months before my release date. That is a long time! My living location was changed around 2 months before my release date. Parole officers need to check where you are living, so this was a big deal. Keep in mind that you want to do your best to ask the officer if they could arrive in dress down clothing when they come for a home inspection. *I learned this the hard way.*

Put yourself in my position: Here I was, finally free. No one in the neighborhood knew my history. Then 2 officers showed up in an all-black Crown Victoria, wearing black shirts and bulletproof vests with big block white letters saying ORANGE COUNTY PROBATION. Yep, if I wanted to be low key, that just went out the window.

Mind you, they did this all knowing that I was living with my son and future daughter-in-law. This was in a 2-month-old new home, in a quiet residential community.

This was great, just great. I was surprised that the officers didn't go knocking on every neighbor's door, flashing a warning sign. Two officers walked in and sat me down in the kitchen. They did not handcuff me (Praise God). One stayed with me the entire time while the other went upstairs to search the bedroom. A very pleasant experience. "NOT!" The next month they did transfer my case to Lake Forest, and I had to meet another probation officer for the first time. Fortunately, this officer was much more down to earth. He, too, needed to visit the home, but he came in shorts and a T-shirt and looked like a member of the family. Officer Z was respectful and did his best not to do anything that would hinder the transition process.

So here is my word to the wise:
- don't commit violations
- follow the rules
- don't play the system
- if, perchance, you are stopped by the police for any reason during your probation period, immediately tell the officer who is stopping you that you are on probation or parole (and

soon as the experience is over, always contact your probation officer immediately to let him know what just happened)

Probation/Parole does not like surprises. Doing the right thing pays off. In many counties, they now use kiosk check-ins where you don't even have to see your officer. This is the lowest form of custody during your probation. My probation officer would have recommended me to do this, but the kiosks were in Santa Ana. It would take me an hour by bus to get there— and an hour to get back. It was just a lot simpler going down to the local station, which was within walking distance from where I lived. If you live near a local kiosk check-in point, request it. If you're doing the right thing, there's no reason why they wouldn't make it easier on you. Be patient. You need to prove to the officer that you are worthy of his or her trust, and that takes a little time. Like with all new relationships, don't rush it or try to push it. Follow the rules. It all falls into place naturally. Getting a job, clean drug tests, and volunteering really go a long way in this situation.

Establishing your banking relationship: You **do** want to disclose your criminal history to your banker. Be upfront and honest. It will pay off big time. Remember, you do not actively disclose your criminal history to your potential landlords or employers. Other former inmates and I have found, through practical experience, that being upfront with your bank is a must. Tell them your story. Thus far, we have had great success with Chase Bank and Union Bank and poor experiences with Wells Fargo. When we wanted to do business with Wells Fargo, they themselves were under criminal investigation. They were doing their best to earn the public's trust back. For whatever reason, they would not open our business or personal accounts. I realize that this information is limited only to my own experience and a few others that I interviewed while writing the book. But I can tell you that both Chase and Union helped set up the right account for the size of the deposits. They took the time to explain everything and had our backs when someone or something was trying to attempt to collect. At this time, you need all the help you can get, and our experience has shown positive results with Chase and Union. PS …..no, they did not pay me to say that.

The value of volunteering: All beginnings require that you unlock new doors. The key to unlocking those new doors is giving and doing. Money is not needed; give charity and do kindness. If you don't have a job lined up, or even if you do, waste no time. Go to any job website and type in the word "volunteer". Let's face it, being a felon is not the best ticket to getting a job, even if you're talented. You need to prove your worth and that now you are a much better person— a different person than what you were before. You need to prove that you're honest, reliable, dependable, and easy to work with. So by volunteering, you can do all that and show that your actions speak as loud as your words.

There are all kinds of things that you can volunteer for. I chose the Saddleback Church food pantry because it was within walking distance from my son's home, and **I did not have to go through a background check**. That's key: no background check means no long explanations. You can do the job. Do it really well, and people will value what you do by your actions. That's a ticket! Of course, the downside is that you are not being paid. Still, it's not really a downside at all. It's giving freely, doing good, and yes, there may be a benefit in the end, but that is for God to decide.

At the Saddleback Church, I heard about a pastor named Rick Warren and the tremendous work he has been doing. He has even visited many prisons throughout California. I had the feeling that it was a natural fit, and the job was helping the Saddleback Ministry to feed the needy and to help people find a spiritual foundation. The Saddleback Church Pantry Shoppers, as they are called, are the volunteers that walk down the isles, helping people shop for their food. But in addition to finding food, they help people find hope by rebuilding their trust in God. I was not a shopper, I was a deckhand, refilling shelves and sorting the donated food coming in on the daily trucks from Costco and Ralphs. Whatever task you are assigned to do as a volunteer, be sure to volunteer for all the right reasons (generosity, kindness, and charity). Put your trust in the Lord, do the right thing, and have some patience. The rest will just happen naturally. So go to all the job sites and type in the word "volunteer". Get started building a new family of friends who will step up for you and confirm how conscientious you are and what a great person you are to work with.

Preparing for your first job interview: You never get a second chance to make a first impression. So the basics are essential: the collars should always match the cuffs. Carefully review the job that you are interested in. Let's say it's a sales job where you will be talking to the public, selling a product. You would need a sports jacket, no jeans, a clean hair cut, a clean and neat face, a shower, a resume, your identification documents in a neat wallet, a freshly shined pair of shoes. To get prepared mentally, always have money in your wallet. You should never go to an interview without cash, even if you have to go to the bank and make a withdrawal (this is a mental thing). Now, you are almost ready to meet your interviewer. Just before you enter the location for the interview, clear your mind, and close your eyes. Repeat to yourself, "I am going to be the best for myself, for my family, and for the company." Repeat it three times, open your eyes and walk in and knock 'em dead.

Your attitude should be humble, but humble doesn't mean "humiliation." Be like Moses in the Bible, who was described as the most humble person on earth, and yet he stood toe-to-toe with Pharaoh. Humble means don't be arrogant and don't be so low that a worm stands above you. Occupy your space. You are strong. You are willing to learn. You desire to be the best. You are a team player, and you're looking to better yourself.

Don't forget to interview the interviewer. Ask questions about the company. Bring a note pad and ask the interviewer if it would be alright to take some notes. After all, this is not your only interview, and you're the type of person who likes to stay organized. Organized, clean looking, and in the moment. Don't worry if you blow it. It doesn't matter. There are tons of job opportunities out there. It is just a numbers game. Go for it!

Follow the same strategy for jobs that are not sales related, such as construction. Make sure that the collars match the cuffs. Jeans works with a button-down shirt, clean looking boots, or shoes. No running shoes. Everything else is the same. A clean cowboy look works really well here.

CHAPTER 8

Employment vs Self-Employment

Seeking Employment: You would think that being upfront and telling your prospective employer about your criminal history would be the right thing to do and the best way of handling your prospective employment. I mean, you're supposed to be rehabilitated. But in reality, it just doesn't work that way. So the approach I'm suggesting is not to lie, but don't volunteer information. If you do, you will be immediately prejudged, and you will rarely get that job. You are under no obligation to give your criminal history upfront. You have protective status, which allows you to do as we discussed in the previous chapter. Your goal is to get in the door, come work early, leave late, don't complain, and be the best you can be. Show management that you are not only capable of doing the work, but that you do an excellent job and are a value to the business. If by chance, a few weeks down the road, someone finds out about your history, they are more likely to overlook your situation.

I can tell you from personal experience, I've tried it both ways deliberately for the benefit of writing this book. **Do not be upfront**. If you are upfront, you will not get the job. Or if you do get one, you will be treated as if it's the biggest favor you ever had in your life and reminded of it all the time. Show them you can do the job. That's what matters most.

Also, some bogus documents are floating around jails and prisons about felon friendly employers. Don't buy them. They are just not real. Employers are friendly to people who can do a job right, and who can profit and benefit by hiring you. The only way to prove that is by doing it— and not just the first week or two. I mean consistently and all the time. For some reason, people tend to work hard the first few weeks on the job, then they get comfortable, slack off, and show their real colors. You should be excited about your work and self-motivated to be the best. Like in horse racing, you need to be strong out of the gate and strong down in the stretch.

But all of this is meaningless if you don't get the chance... So remember, actions speak louder than words. You need to walk your talk and be prepared to work towards being the best. Like I tell my children, "You work hard, and good things happen."

Today, job searching is usually done via the internet. And yes, there are numerous apps to use on the phone. It's a numbers game. Prepare to do battle. At some point, you're going to have to explain your criminal record when asked a direct question. It is a matter of when not if. Prepare your resumé, do your interviews, and get the job (or at least a conditional job offer). Then if your background is checked, I believe there are two approaches. One is the rehabilitation approach. This is basically telling your prospective employer that you made a mistake, that you learned your lesson, and why the company will benefit by hiring you. The second approach is to tell your prospective employer that your case is still a work in progress, and the criminal conviction is not at all related to what the employment tasks require. I have attached my responses to Home Depot Human Resources and Mother's Market inquiries regarding my criminal record as an example for you. By the way, Home Depot is **NOT** a Felon Friendly Employer. Also, realize that these were for entry-level clerical positions.

On Wed, Apr 18, 2018 at 1:43 PM <mythdhr@homedepot.com> wrote:
Hello,
The Home Depot has received the results of your background report and needs additional information regarding the information contained in the report. Please enter detailed responses below each question for each charge/conviction noted and send your response back by replying to this email or fax to 1-877-959-8144.
List of charges/convictions:
1. GRAND THEFT 4 COUNT

Ticket #: 23547374

This was my response:

APPROACH (Work in progress)

It's complicated but I will try and simplify. I had never been in trouble my entire life. I left my career as a Certified Financial Planner to go into business with a former client. The business failed and I was held to blame. I went to court and lost "September 29th, 2014" and sentenced to 9.4 years in State Prison. The crime was centered around self directed retirement trusts, that are financially very complicated.. I am still in the process of having all the charges thrown out on the Federal level as a mistrial. Regardless, I'm sorry for what happened and will be spending the rest of my life trying to make amends.

I served a little over three years, most of which was served in a conservation camp fighting California wildfires. My position at camp was a Butcher working 12 hours a day, 7 days a week.

I was released February 8, 2018 because of good behavior and am currently on probation. My probation officer has given me a green light to work at Home Depot. The probation office is two blocks from the store.

But all of this has really no affect on my ability to work at Home Depot. I want to work, and get back into a routine. It's not the money, my retirement pension kicks in June. I can contribute to Home Depot and who knows, you never know where opportunities lead. My family and friends have been major customers for years. In fact their purchases will be tenfold over what I'm going to be paid.

With great humility I'm asking for a break. You won't lose dime. In fact, it's a win win. You'll have an associate with 45 years of business experience, college educated, and experienced in customer service for your patrons. I am a person who takes the time to carefully listen to customers needs. For me this is a place to go and be part of a team again. My work ethic is old school as well as my confidentiality. I'm a company man. If I'm not a good fit, I'll leave, no questions asked. Right now I'm working at the local church as a volunteer (a total give back).

Humbly and Respectfully,
Robert Barth

APPROACH (Rehabilitation)

Here's a different approach created by my daughter Symphony. Her logic was that you're not in court anymore and there's nothing to defend. Stop trying to justify the past and show that you're a different person. So here is her response written for me.

To: Accurate Background
7515 Irvine Center Drive
Irvine, CA 92618
customer_service@accuratebackground.com
800-784-3911

Dear Accurate Background,

I am writing this letter to be given the opportunity to work at Mother's Market Laguna Hills. In September of 2014, I was convicted of Securities Misrepresentation, a non-violent white collar crime and due to this I received a state prison sentence of 9.4 years. I was granted the opportunity to join fire camp and worked there as a Butcher. I was then moved to the Sierra Conservation Center where I finished my sentence in a little over 3 years. After this, I moved back to Southern California where I currently live with my son and his fiancée.

Since my return home, I have spent countless hours re-establishing my relationships with friends and family and helping the needy as a volunteer at the Saddleback Church Food Pantry. The Food Pantry at the Saddleback Church Peace Center has been a great opportunity for me as I have been able to get myself back into the community and at the same time enjoy the experience of giving back. For that I am grateful.

With that being said, working at Mother's Market Laguna Hills will give me the opportunity to get back to being a productive member of society and the community. To do this I will be able to use my 45 plus years of business experience to accommodate customers and to exceed their expectations every time, thus building loyalty and patronage. In addition, I've got years of experience working everything from Front End, Deli, Meat,

Dairy and Frozen Foods and can use those skills to be the best employee.

Finally, I work everyday intellectually and spiritually to be a better person continuing to progress in my ability to rehabilitate myself into society. I will state that this opportunity will not only allow me to better myself, but also to better my family and community. I am a 66 year old man, that understands the gravity of my case and am asking to be granted to ability to show that I can be better. My family is my most important goal and I would like to show my three children that I can be better for all of us. I hope that you are able to grant me this opportunity; so that I can be the person I know I was meant to be.

Sincerely, Robert Barth

Be prepared for lots of work and lots of energy in your attempts to find employment. Home Depot sent a cleaver letter and told me they will not hire me. Because they gave me a conditional offer, I had the right to file a complaint with the State. I don't know how you feel about filing complaints, but I'm tired of legal actions. Filing a complaint was like filing another worthless 602 Form. Mother's Market said "no" as well. I did get a job... a great job working for a smaller company. It is much, much better than Home Depot and Mother's Market combined! And guess what? I got this job because the owner was a member connected to the Saddleback Church. He called the supervisor at the pantry, where I volunteered, and the rest was history. The value of volunteering is priceless, and it was totally unexpected. Answered Prayer! Pray for whatever you need, God is listening.

Now if you can get past the false sense of security from working for someone else...

TIME TO BE YOUR OWN BOSS!

Going into business for yourself is a lot easier than most people think. All you need is a hard work ethic and the desire not to do a *good* job, but the desire to do a *great* job— a job that will exceed the customers' expectations. Although you never want to promise more than you can deliver, once you have agreed upon whatever service or product you are offering, you want to surprise them by going over and above the expectation. That's the secret of success in keeping and retaining good customers. You also need to be a good Boy Scout all the time. Never lie and always charge a fair and marketable price for your service or product. If you can do all that, then the rest of it is just a numbers game and a stick-to-it attitude. Oh, yeah, there is one more thing you will need to get used to hearing the words no, no, no, no, no, no, no, no, YES! No matter what you do or sell, most people are inclined to be set in their ways. This is actually a good thing because that means that most of your customers will stay loyal for a period of time. That's how businesses are built.

You should give a lot of thought and consideration to starting your own business. If you need a little safety net, use a combination strategy, and work for an employer and have your own business, too. To me, doing that is like learning how to swim with one leg still outside the pool. I personally jump in and get wet. It's not going to be perfect by any means, but that's real life. It's not that hard, and you can make almost anything into a business. Washing windows, pick-up and delivery, pool cleaning, catering, house cleaning, junk removal, sign making, marketing and demonstrating, graphic arts, etc. It's endless, really. Although there are a few exceptions, most people don't do a criminal background check on someone selling hot dogs, chips, and pop on the corner. They usually don't check auto detailers or even the gardeners. All it takes is a business card, checking account, a warm smile, and a sincere desire to help people. You have to do a quality job, giving people more than what is expected and a reason for choosing you. Yes, there's a little more to it, but that's one of the reasons I wrote this book. First, you need to know how much money you need to earn, then you can do the easy math.

Let's first examine the benefits of being self-employed. It is so much better than working for someone else. There are lots of reasons, but I picked out the standouts.

The 12 Best Reasons To Be Self-Employed Rather Than An Employee

1. **You're your own boss.** You knew this one was coming, didn't you? It's the one we all dreamed about when we realized self-employment was a viable option: being our own boss. Here's to escaping the rat race and living life as we please! Remember that? When you're self-employed, you no longer have a "higher-up" governing your every move. You control how your work is done. Your customer has a say in the final product, but that's it — their power ends there. How you get from point A to point B is completely up to you— and that is awesome.

2. **You earn more money.** On average, those who are self-employed earn 45% more than those who are traditionally employed. 45%— that's not 10%. That's not 20%. It's **45%!** The self-employed are also allowed to deduct certain business expenses that employees are not, which allows them to keep more of what they earn. Go back and see the sample chart in the beginning sections "Why People Fail Financially" (see page 39). Do you feel like you're not quite there yet? One of my fellow inmates decided to start a pool cleaning business. With no exaggeration, he has 40 customers in 3 months. Each customer paid an average of $150/month. That's $6000/month! He works hard, and he is busy all the time. But

it's ten times better than getting that middle of the night warehouse job for $12 an hour at UPS. There's no reason you can't pull in just as much (or more!) now than you did before all this mess started for you.

3. **You spend less.** Are you better working in an office? When was the last time you were stuck in traffic on your way to work? If you can perform your professional duties from a home office, you can make a business out of it. Think of all the money on gas you'd be saving. Even if you work outside of your home, as someone self-employed, you can choose the location. And I'd be willing to bet you choose somewhere that nixed the lengthy commute. Childcare expenses can also be a thing of the past for you, along with expensive daily lunches "out" because of your distinct distrust of the office fridge.

4. **You enjoy variety.** When you were an employee — whether you were crumbling away in a cubicle, restlessly working retail, or dying at the drive-thru — you were handed a manual or given some hasty instructions by your boss. And then...that was it. You knew what you needed to know to perform your job, and there was never any reason to grow beyond that. Your job never ever changed. When you are self-employed, your job is constantly changing. You're expected to adapt, learn, and update your skills. With every new customer comes a new challenge. When

you're self-employed, you're forced to think — to be creative — and you love it, don't you? (It's okay to admit it. Go ahead. Take a second to say it out loud.). It's a great feeling to know that your skills are being put to good use and that those skills are going to continue to grow as your business grows.

5. **No co-worker drama.** Many of us work alone (or work remotely) and that isolation can be a bit daunting at times. But do you really, honestly, miss your co-workers? Even the one who listened to their music on headphones? Or the guy who loved to talk (loudly) on his cell phone during his breaks...right next to you? Or how about the gem of a human being who shirked all of their cleaning duties on you? Your favorite co-workers became your friends and are likely still a part of your life in that capacity. Everyone else? Good riddance!

6. **Sick Day? A-OK!** I knew a freelance writer who has been self-employed for so long that she was taken aback when, upon a recent visit to the hospital, she was asked if she needed a note excusing the absence. She said, "And then I realize[d] that the default method in the world of work and education is to treat people as if they are incompetent or lying or both. Because that's the only explanation for what is clearly a routine question for an exam during business hours. I guess if I were employed in the traditional corporate

world, I'd be forced to ask, 'Please, boss, can I take my daughter to see the neurosurgeon? No? Okay.' Seriously? Seriously?" A day we don't work is a day we go without pay, but at least we can take that day off without having to beg for our boss' forgiveness. Or feel the demeaning sting of having to prove how ill we were by providing a doctor's note. Or fill out a stack of meaningless forms. Of course, we eventually have to buy our own health insurance. But not if you're being released from prison. The state provides coverage during your parole. One year later, eventually, you get to choose which insurance you want to use. But even this is better than having your health coverage left up to a head honcho choosing the cheapest package.

7. **Your work area is truly yours.** Want dual monitors instead of one? Go ahead. Prefer a standing desk? Knock yourself out. And framed photos of your friends and family? The more, the merrier! Decoration regulations (try saying that ten times fast!) are a thing of the past. You can Feng Shui your workspace to your heart's content. So put up that poster you found online, get in the habit of watering your indoor fern, and finally buy that ergonomically correct chair!

Need some inspiration? Have faith. Believe in the fact that God will provide. Just pick out a business and get ready to hear no, no, no, no, no, no then the YES! That's the reality of it. Most people are reluctant to change, which is a good thing because once you earn a new customer, you certainly don't want them switching hats every day. It's a numbers game. When you hear the no, just say thank you with a smile and ask them to keep your card for future consideration. Grandma Anne (99 years old, God bless her soul) sold insurance for most of her adult life. She retired in her 90's. She said she used to keep 10 pennies in her right pocket and move a penny from her right pocket to her left every time she heard the word "no." She would keep the pennies in her right pocket for the yes's. At the end of the day, in her right pocket, she always had one or two, maybe three, if she really had a good day. Whatever system you use, believe me, there's value in everything you do in business, even the no's. Put the effort in and have some faith, and God will provide.

8. **New equipment when you want/need it.** If you've ever worked in an office building, you're well aware of the frustrations that come along with the I-need-something hierarchy. Whether you need a new pack of pens, staples, or laptop repair, as an employee, you would have to ask someone for the equipment you needed. And then they would ask someone else, who would ask someone else, who would ask someone else. It could take anywhere from a few hours to a few weeks to get the equipment or maintenance you

needed to complete your project. As your own boss, if you need something, you simply go to the store and get it. Get back to work. The end.

9. **No uniforms, unless you want them.** Being self-employed is a bit like being Phil Collins: No Jacket Required. Of course, if you're meeting with a client or customer in person — or via video chat — you can wear (or not wear) whatever you darn well please. It might be a cliche to freelance in the buff, but it's definitely an option.

10. **You set your own schedule.** Whether you crave the steady familiarity of a fixed schedule or you long to mix it up with hours that are more flexible, as your own boss, you're the one who creates your schedule. If you're not a morning person, you can rest easy knowing that you no longer have to set your alarms in triplicate to just barely make your morning meeting. Or, if early morning is your style, you can set your hours for the dawn and have a full day's work done before your kids get up for school.

11. **You're more valued.** As an owner, you're no longer part of the hive; you're a highly-valued individual. More importantly, you get to decide what that value is through a well-devised proposal like this one. You get credit for your own work. And, through your ongoing marketing efforts, you've even started to earn some name recognition, not just among your long-time clients, but from complete strangers as well.

12. You choose your own customers. When you work as an employee, you're more-or-less forced to serve whoever decides to show up at your employer's place of business. Whether it's a bedraggled couple with two crying children looking to buy school supplies or the old man who screams at you because he still hasn't quite figured out how the combo menu works or the confused woman who's called three times in the past hour with the exact same customer service question: you had to help them. Because that was your job. If a customer yells at you now, it's because you chose the wrong customer. You're the one in control now, not them. You choose who you provide services to.

The Final Word on Self-Employment. You can turn almost anything into a business— your own business. While in custody, just start thinking and planning. When I was doing my jail time, I met a young man, Jim, in custody for a probation violation. He shared his story with me. I found out that before his incarceration, he was a mechanic working for General Motors. He was one of the "The Good Guys." Upon his release, his father was willing to lend him his truck and a garage full of professional automotive repair and servicing tools. Together we created a business plan to service automobiles right at people's homes.

We did all the things mentioned in this book: figured out how much money he needed (The X's), established goals and objectives, etc. I also explained to him that people who work for a living, who have long commutes going back and forth to work all week long, come home for the weekend and the last thing they want to do is get back into the car and drive to the service station for the oil change and filter. We designed a business plan whereby Jim went to the customer's home, with the oil, filters, etc. He brought all the tools and did the oil change right in their driveway. He worked so clean and fast that you would never know he was there. And because he doesn't have to pay rent for a service station, he can charge less than even the quick lube places. 90% of his customers pay him cash! Don't ever forget, when anyone asks if you accept cash, always respond, "Cash is King!" His business is booming!

The key is to make sure that whatever it is you want to do has the capacity to earn the income that you require. It's also a really big plus to design a business plan like Jim's, where you can set it up for repeat customers, so you are not having to wait for a phone call, and you can set up service routes. Go check your numbers already written down, in quadrant II for the first 6 months, 7-18th months, and 18th and beyond. That's what you need to make, now think of what you can do to make it.

Yep, sometimes while being in your own business, the stress of everyday life can start to wear thin on you, and you forget how amazing your life really is — being in your own business. You may even consider for a split second (or more) about giving it all up from time to time. **The truth is, reality jumps in and smacks you right in the head. Are You Nuts! Self-employment is a fantastic lifestyle choice. You are starting over anyhow, just do it!**

Build "starting your own business" into your plan by working backward, calculate the amount of money you need (e.g., $4000/month). For example, with auto detailing, by working 5 days a week, you would need $200/day. So that can be 2 autos at $100 or 4 autos at $50 or 8 autos at $25. Each one of those generates $200/day, and that is only working 5 days each week. Kill all the negative thoughts. "There are so many people in that business, do people really need auto detailing?" Forget all that nonsense thinking. You don't need a corporation or anything fancy. All you need is a checking account with your name on it and a business card, maybe print a flyer. **Then the only thing left to do, get yourself 10 pennies and put them in your right pocket and go out and let people know what you do. Then do a great job and get used to no, no, no, no, no, no, no, no, no, YES!**

CHAPTER 9

Purchasing a Home for Little or No Money Down

You can buy a home for little or no money down. You don't need to buy a book on how to do it. While you're in custody with nothing but time on your hands, there is no reason why you can't buy a few books or go to the library and start getting familiar with real estate terms.

I am going to attempt to make this as simple as possible. I've always been a believer that when things are simple and make common sense, they do just that. So we are going to try to keep this as simple as possible. Even better, the internet and social media have made locating opportunity properties easier than ever before. Yes, your iPhone has an app for that, too. What an amazing tool! The iPhone is a trusted Artificial Intelligence partner right in your pocket! If this was 40 years ago and you said something like that, you would think it was like a science fiction movie, almost alien in nature, "There's a creature in my pocket! Artificial Intelligence!" But it's just another one of the Lord's beautiful creations. He gives us the free will and ability to use this remarkable tool for good.

Let's start by saying that buying a house is a major purchase, and it's a very important one. Some folks talk about buying homes like they were buying a car. Let's not belittle it. This is an important decision, especially for those who are coming out of custody and rebuilding their life. Owning a home is all part of the second chance. In my opinion, buying a home is critical to your rehabilitation. You won't screw up because you have your own place. It's your investment, and it's all wrapped into one. A house can be used for enjoyment now, and it is an asset to sell in the future. A house can be rented to others to generate income. But more importantly, owning a home is something you work for. It fills you with pride of ownership, making you a solid member of your community. Once you have a home, there's no going back. You *get out and stay out.*

It's critical that the house you purchase be affordable. And I mean really affordable. Too much home can mean too much financial burden. One of the top reasons people get a divorce is too much house. People become house poor and can't enjoy life. Life becomes unbalanced, as we discussed before. Unbalanced doesn't work. But remember, you are only looking to acquire the home after you have your E-Fund in place. You have the cash available for any minimal down payment and escrow expenses. And you have established income equal to or greater than the projected amount listed after the 36th month. *Now it just feels right.* You have a really good understanding of what is going on in your life— personally, spiritually, how this acquisition will affect your family and friends, and the impact to your business goals.

After all of what I have said, you may be asking why so many people rent. For one, they think they can't afford to purchase a house, or they just don't know, or their family has always rented, or homeownership freaks them out. If you don't own a home, ask yourself why. You do need to have some confidence. But it's the same confidence you needed to overcome the items we discussed at the beginning of the book, under Why People Fail— why people get stressed out over financial issues to the point of disability.

But things have now changed since the beginning of this book— you have changed! You now know or have been thinking seriously about your cash flow. You now know what you need, and you have taken the time to write it down in a plan. A home purchase, for most of us, is not going to be acted upon until you have accomplished most of your goals. If you are like me, starting from scratch, it's highly recommended that you wait until you are near the 36th-month mark. That doesn't mean you can't plan for it or learn about it or talk about it or get ready for it. In fact, that's what you should be doing. That's the important work, "The B's." Plus, you will be maximizing your time while in custody.

Don't worry about the availability of houses. There is always a deal to be found. If the process I am about to describe starts to overwhelm you, by all means, wait. Find a good agent and take that route or reach out to me at GHE Publishing. We have our contact information in the back of the book. Buying a house is not that complicated. You can and will be able to do it all by yourself. You will see why very shortly.

The other thing about buying real estate with little or no money down is that you should not expect it to be a quick purchase. If it were that easy, everyone and anyone would be doing it. Think of this as if you open a savings account down the street from your house at the bank. Most of the time, it's really easy to do. You can open an account with very little money. But the fees are high, and they pay the least amount of interest on your money. But if you put in some effort and go out and start shopping around for a bank, you will find banks online or maybe out of state that have lower or no fees— and pay out higher interest.

It's the same money, your money. It's the same FDIC insurance. All you had to do was work a little harder. Remember: Work hard, good things happen. Same thing, the easy way to buy a house, put 20% down, have good credit and a good job, and you're going to have a standard mortgage and a standard deal. But that's not what we have here. We are starting over. We want the least amount of money out of pocket. We shop around and find the right deal, put in the effort, and bring that puppy home.

Here's a warning: you can't allow yourself to get too emotionally involved. Don't fall in love here. That's not a good thing. You can love many houses. That doesn't make it your soul mate. This is a house. Let's try and keep that all together. This is really important, especially if you are married. It's really tough to make an intelligent financial decision when your significant other is turning an important business transaction into mission impossible: "Honey, I want this house!" Or how about this: "If you love me, you will do this for me." Oh, please, spare me. We need to let that go. I'm not saying it's a bad thing. It's better to realize that it really doesn't matter. The Lord will provide. You do the work, and the rest will happen naturally. The Lord will make it an easy process. Be prepared for work. It is going to take some time and a lot of effort. You have to research all of this. But the fact is, anything that's really worth something does take work and effort. I also believe that if you do the work, the Lord will do the rest.

The quality of the house you will find when researching homes with the potential of little or no down payment, really reflects the current market conditions. If the housing market is a seller's market (little inventory and lots of buyers and few sellers), then sellers have the edge. It's not that there aren't any homes available. There are always homes available with special terms. But it's harder to find special deal properties with lots of bells and whistles.

But in a buyer's market, it's a whole other story. There's lots of inventory and lots of premium properties with all kinds of bells and whistles. In fact, there are so many properties available that they become tougher to sell, and they sit on the market for weeks, months, and sometimes years. Many sellers have such a tough time selling their property that they don't want the internet to know that the home has been on the market for a year. What do they do? Many of them take the property off the market and then place it back on the market repeatedly, attempting to make it look like it's only been on the market for a few days. I do a lot of walking and jogging in neighborhoods. I can't get over how many signs say "Just Listed OPEN HOUSE," but that sign has been up for the past 6 months! The main reason sales are slow in a buyer's market is that the traditional buyers and prime buyers (20% down with rock-solid credit) want the price reduced. They have the cash and the perfect credit. And they are already pre-approved by the lenders. That fact, in and of itself, creates the opportunity for you.

Since sellers may have invested lots of money trying to flip the house, they want out of the house, but they can't drop the price. They need to sell it for a specific price, or they will be losing money. You, on the other hand, are not a home flipper (at least not yet), and you are not that interested in the best for the cheapest. That would be nice, but when you don't have the money or the credit score, the price is not as important as the **terms**. Let me say that again: when you don't have the money, the price is not as important as the **terms.** The terms have value! Your goal is to have an affordable home that you can own. That's the goal. It's a long-term goal. You are not looking to flip the house. You are looking to acquire it, live in it long-term, maintain it, build friendships with neighbors, maybe even raise a family. Regardless of whether it is a buyer's market or seller's market, there's always someone who needs to sell a home.

Let's put aside the strategies for a second and look at the basic components of the home acquisition. Obviously, at this point, you have the property you want to purchase. It's not just any property, you're thinking single-family home— could be a condo or a townhome. From experience, detached single-family homes seem to be the ticket. The second component is a promissory note. You are not buying the house outright with cash. And since you are not buying the house outright with cash, you are going to have to promise to pay someone. That someone could be the bank, mortgage banker, the homeowner, a company, or an interested third party. That promise to pay is a modified IOU. An IOU (from the phrase "I owe you") is usually an informal document acknowledging the debt. An IOU differs from a promissory note in that an IOU is not a negotiable instrument and does not specify repayment terms such as the time of repayment. On the other hand, the promissory note is a written note which describes how you promise to pay, **which can be very creative**. That's worth repeating: a promissory note, which is a promise to pay, **can be very creative**.

Generally, when you buy a house, the lender gives you a schedule for the repayment of the loan. This schedule is a series of payments that include principal and interest, called an "amortization schedule." But let's stop right here and think about it. Terms of a promissory note can be almost any terms you want them to be as long as both parties agree. Let's say you create a note that states, "I'm going to give you $1000 down today and 12 months from now, I will start paying $1500 a month for the next 60 months, then skip a year and then start paying again." It's all good as long as both parties agree. Now, in general, when banks are involved, they dictate the terms. But when an owner of the property finances the deal, any and all terms can be on the table. So when banks are removed from the transaction, and the seller is the one providing the financing, anything goes. Once the buyer and seller have scratched it out on paper and all the terms are agreed upon, you just get the money to an **ESCROW, and they will do the rest**. Escrow is a key Component. We will cover this very important component of the transaction shortly. Let's move on for now.

Who is going to accept the promise of a stranger? Not many people. That is the reason the promise (Promissory Note) has to be secured. The security instrument is known as a "Deed of Trust." In real estate in the United States, a **Deed of Trust** is essentially an agreement between a lender and a borrower to give the title to the property to a neutral third party who will serve as a trustee. The trustee holds the title of the property until the borrower pays off the debt. The equitable title (the power to sell, maintain, borrow against etc.) remains with the borrower, but if you don't do what you promise to do, in simplistic terms, you lose the property. Makes sense? That security device is called a Trust Deed, aka Deed of Trust. Most people never have the title to their home unless it is paid off in full. Most people just have the right to sell their home. That's all. And if you fail to pay your monthly installments, that right reverts back to the holder or trustee, which in most cases is a Title Company. That process is called foreclosure. It's not a good thing most of the time. The Trust Deed or Deed of Trust is the third component.

"Terms" is the next component. It's really important that your offer only includes terms that you can afford. For instance, let's say you are renting right now and paying $2000/month. It's financially comfortable. In addition, you are doing everything you planned on doing, searching the web, checking the newspapers. Then suddenly, you find a home. The owner of that home owns the house outright. He and his wife are looking to retire in Florida. They have lived in this house all their life. There was a big sign out in front that said *FOR SALE BY OWNER*. You took the time to meet them and went back a few times to visit. Maybe in the course of conversation, you shared a little about your life, and they shared a little about their life. They like you and really would like you to have the house because they feel that you will treat it the way it has treated them for all these years. The house was more than just a house— it was a blessing. This is where they raised their family, who are now all grown up. The homeowner has meticulously cared for the house. But the price is high compared to other similar properties in the area— $20,000 more than any other home in the area. The owner needs the money for his retirement and needs to sell the house for $200,000. They don't need the cash upfront, what they need is an income stream, a monthly check. If you did a conventional financing 30-year mortgage, you would be putting down $40,000 and financing a mortgage from a bank for around $764 (which includes principal and interest). Then throw in taxes and insurance, and it would all add up to $1200/month.

In this situation, you would be a prime buyer, and let's face it, right now, you are not a prime buyer. If you were, you would not be paying top dollar. If for some reason you did buy the home at the full cash price, the seller is going to end up with a lot less in their pocket after taxes.

But there is a better option. You and the owner get together and have a chat. You agree to buy the home for $200,000 and offer to pay $2000/month with the seller financing everything. With this agreement, $400/month goes into an escrow account to pay for taxes and insurance. The additional $600/month goes to the seller, paying part of the down payment. Plus, there is a $1000 payment for principal and interest at a fair market rate. You get a premium house, the owner gets his monthly retirement and, guess what, *No Down Payment*!

Let's use the same logic, but this time the seller would like to be cashed out some point. So with this second option, for the same $2000/month, you set the promissory note up for 5 years instead of 30 years of principal and interest payments. At the end of 5 years, you could go to the bank and take out a mortgage using all the $600 per month payments over the 5 years as your down payment. That's $36,000. Or just keep going with the agreement until another agreed-upon point in time. For you, you now have pride of ownership with little or no money out of pocket. You are a happy camper. You have your own home with no money out of pocket. The seller is a happy camper. The seller is getting $1600/month to supplement his retirement and social security— and it's income tax efficient. This is a beautiful deal, and America is a great country. Everybody wins.

So let's recap the components at this point, we have the property, promissory note, deed of trust, and the terms. Now, this is really important, we need *escrow*. What the hell is escrow? No, it's not a mixed green that you put in a salad. Nope, the best way to make it easy to understand escrow is how I learned about it at Mr. John Stapleton's School of Real Estate in Honolulu, Hawaii. John Stapleton is a great real estate educator. I still remember what he told me— this was back in 1987. He said that when you think of escrow, think of an old western movie. You are in the saloon, and there are guys playing poker, women selling dances for a nickel, and old Gabby the drunk on the floor in the corner. There's an argument at the poker table. One gunslinger is calling the other gunslinger a cheat. They settle it by gunfight, each of them gives up a $100 gold piece. The winner gets all. So they take their money out and hand it off to Gabby, who is as drunk as a skunk in the corner. But, he is an impartial third party. He does not care who lives or dies, he just wants to get paid $5 for holding the money while these guys try to kill each other for $100. Gabby the drunk is the impartial third party— Gabby is Escrow. Escrow writes and prepares the promissory notes and deeds of trust. Escrow arranges the home inspections, pest inspections, and title insurance. In fact, escrow does all the things you do not have to remember to do because you pay escrow to do it. Escrow is like Gabby, only most of the time not as drunk. In short, escrow's job is to transact the house as agreed lawfully from party A to B and take care of all the details to protect all interested parties. Escrow is a key component.

Now, we could go on and on, over each item listed in the real estate deal, such as title insurance and so on, but I'm not going to. You can go to the Prison library or have family send in books to study. All you really need to know is that escrow knows what to do. So when you have an agreement between buyer and seller over a piece of real estate, it's time to get out your checkbook and find an escrow company to do the work. The term used is "Open Escrow."

If you sit down with the escrow officer, he or she will explain all the agreed terms and put the deal together. He or she will give everyone a package of paperwork to sign. Then you sign, the money is paid, and that's called "The Closing." The deal is done.

Other Strategies and Scenarios

Okay, let's say the same seller had some remaining financing on the property with the bank. You can still do the same deal with the same $2000, and you don't have to pay off that loan. Keep the financing in place and buy the property "Subject To" the existing financing. In this case, you make the check payable to the title company, the "real owner" of the property, or a mortgage servicing company. They pay the bank or mortgage holder, and they make the payments to the seller. They can even pay for taxes and insurance! Everybody wins: the seller sells the home, the buyer gets the home, the title changes. The seller does have a little exposure if you default because the property is coming back. But it's no more exposure than the previous two we discussed. The lender could call in the Due On Sale Clause, but if payments are made, I have never seen it happen. In general, there is very little risk to the seller because most buyers do not want to lose the money they have already put into their home. If, for some reason, you did get into financial trouble that you couldn't get out of (which would be very rare if you are reading this book), you would want to sell the house. Again the house is your responsibility, and it should be— it's your property.

Here are a few other combinations used over my career with great success, but no need to limit yourself here—"anything goes." But remember, if you want the deal to happen, it's got to benefit both sides. This is not a plea deal, where you're being screwed.

If you have a very weak real estate market, or the house is a fixer, try this method. Have the seller-financed interest-only payments for a period of time with principal payment drop-ins. So let's use the case that we just described: you have a motivated seller and limited cash flow right now, but expect your cash flow to be much better down the road. Offer to pay interest-only on the loan. That interest was about $684/month, plus insurance and taxes. You pay the $684 monthly, and at a fixed period of time, you can send the seller $5000, which could be a year down the road. In the meantime, if you were paying $2000 a month in rent, you would have saved more than $12,000 a year. So this method doesn't interrupt your cash flow. Plus, with the money left over, you can put it into future savings or home improvements. Again everyone wins, the house becomes very affordable in the early months of ownership, the seller gets his money, the house is sold, and everyone wins.

Always use kind words when starting your dialogue with the seller. Let the seller know you love the property, and that you want the property. Tell the seller that you either cannot afford the down payment at the moment or that you prefer to hold on to the money for business needs or some other needs. Don't think that by telling the seller you love the house, it's going to cost you. Remember, you are not looking for the lowest price to pay, you are looking for the lowest out of pocket costs. Once your deal is agreed upon, just call your local Escrow "Gabby." Give them a check, and they will open an Escrow for all the interested parties. They will guide you through the process to its completion— otherwise known as "close of escrow."

I know what you're thinking: why would anyone

want to sell a home for little or no money down? That's an excellent question, and I'm glad you asked it. There are many reasons, but let me share some of the main ones. First, understand that, for a seller, this is a smart play. And for the buyer, it is just as smart. That's important because a good deal has value to both buyer and seller. Here are some of the reasons why a seller is motivated to move their property for little or no money down:

A homeowner who found him or herself in custody. That just recently happened no more than 20 minutes away from where I'm typing this. A guy just acquired a beautiful 4000 square foot home. Shortly after that, he was arrested. I don't know what happened, but he took it to trial and lost. They gave him a lot of years. Someone picked up the house on special terms.

Sometimes you have a seller who was **gifted a property they never wanted**. He or she is not around to check on it. Or they just don't have the time to pay bills or fix things up. They want out. Your job is to give them a reason. Be prepared to think through a good deal, how much a month, etc. When you put the energy in, things like this will pop. You need to do the research. You need to communicate, and you will find gold.

Someone decided that they were not cut out for being landlords. They bought a book or attended one of those seminars that teach you how to make millions in real estate. "Not!" It takes a lot more than attending a seminar to get rich in real estate. That lesson is learned first hand when you just signed the property over to the wrong renters— people who have zero respect for other people's property. The wrong renters abuse the property. Sometimes the rental investment did not generate enough positive cash flow. So the investor has to continue to pay, draining his or her cash flow each and every month. For them, it's been a nightmare, and they cannot wait to sell it.

Sensing when an owner wants out is pretty easy. Statements like, "I'm not setting any appointments until I'm sure you're going to be there. Too many times, I'm just sitting there, and no one shows." Or the owner's attitude is just plain grouchy in general when you meet. The more untrusting, non-believing owner that you meet, the easier a low down payment (or no down payment) purchase you can get. But you will have to convince the seller that you are trustworthy. You may even have to visit the property several times, bring the family for their opinion, and become a good friend of the seller.

Rentals that have a tough time renting are great candidates. The seller really wants to get rid of the nightmare and put the house on a one-way trip, but they just don't know how to sell it, get the terms, make a deal and call escrow.

I found lots of construction workers, handymen, and welders in custody. If you are the hands-on type and have no problems getting dirty, there are a ton of fixer houses to be acquired creatively. You have the best reason for putting little or no money down—

you need the money to fix the place up. For people who have a construction or handyman background, these properties are a dream come true. The effort put into repairing and upgrading adds to the future value of the property. If you like the work, you can make it a business too!

An owner was priced out of the market. The seller is faced with a housing market that has dropped and now wants to sell. The problem is that they have put so much money into the property, if they sell at the market price, they will lose big time. So a buyer, offering a creative way to get his asking price, is above market price. The seller is all ears and more motivated to take a hard look at your creative deal. They are motivated for two reasons: they do not want to lose money. And, if you can keep a higher sale price, it serves as a comparable sale for the area. Again both sides benefit. The seller doesn't lose money, and the buyer gains a property (most of the time with a lot of bells and whistles for little or no money out of pocket). Since the buyer is interested in living in the property over the long term, the price doesn't matter as much. Eventually, the property will appreciate and make up the difference... and then some.

A death occurred in the family. Often, a home is left to children who have little or no interest in keeping the house. They are not interested in spending the money to fix things up. But this situation has something other homes don't, sentimental value and family memories. Sometimes the relatives of the deceased would like to see it used for the good, to help others have a happy life. Most of the time, the house is entirely paid off. So the monthly payments from the sale supplement the family income. They are not taking much risk. If there is a default, the property is going to revert back to the estate. You can also be very creative with this type of purchase. By building in a 5-year refinance clause, you can refinance the property and pay the balance in full to the beneficiaries at the end of five years. More than once, I've assisted in this type of purchase. The beautiful part is it turns into a lifelong friendship between buyer and seller. The sentimental value hits home after the house is sold, and the sellers return just to visit the home they were brought up in. This type of situation is not planned; it just happens by the grace of the Lord. Building a relationship with the seller is essential in almost all creative arrangements.

Tax benefits. When people rent their house, the government says it is going to be worth less the following year; it depreciates. (An exception to this is if you improved it some way by adding a deck, for example.) So the tax law allows individuals to deduct an amount each year that represents that depreciation.

So, for example, a house for rent was purchased for $100,000. The *cost basis* is $100,000. At the end of the year, if the property was depreciated by $10,000 for tax purposes, the new basis becomes $90,000 for taxes. If you followed that year after year, what happens when it gets to zero? This is where there is a problem. When this seller decides to sell this property with a zero cost basis for the same $100,000, he has to recognize a $100,000 gain all at once on his taxes. But if he sold that home under contract for 360 payments over 30 years plus interest, the seller only has to recognize the portion of the payments as the gain. A rental property for sale that has been rented for many years has those qualities.

In many cases, the homeowner is not aware of this. By bringing the tax issues to his or her attention, you can create a dialogue that can get you that property for little or no money out of pocket. Always consult a tax professional first.

A house is on the market for a very long time. This situation could happen because the house is a fixer, or the listing price is higher than the cost of the same or similar properties in the area. Sometimes, it's just the wrong location, or it could be a really bad neighbor. Properties that are on the market for long periods are typically priced above the market value. It's not that the seller does not want to sell; it's that they need to sell it a specific price, or they will lose money. They are stubborn, and rightfully so. They invested too much money. The property looks fantastic, but no one wants to buy it— except for you. Instead of selling at a loss and moving on, they choose to be stubborn and not give up. Their stubbornness is your benefit. It is customary to think that you should be shopping for a house at the lowest price. But it is not necessarily the best option when it comes to obtaining properties for little or no money down. Favorable terms add value to you. You're able to take possession without tying up your money in real estate, which leaves money available for other investments or in savings waiting for the next opportunity.

In deals like these, it's highly recommended that the buyer (you) pay for the homeowner's inspection and the termite inspection. Then you should split the remaining escrow fees. The logic here is that the home and termite inspectors will be more critical when the buyer pays the fees. Secondly, these are expenses that sellers typically pay for. So again, it's an upfront olive branch. I mean, after everything is said and done, you are getting a house— a home this is not a birthday gift or a car. This is a home for little or no money out of pocket. If the deal is sweet enough, you may just want to pay for everything, including all the escrow expenses. When you have an owner who is just so sick and tired of the property and of being a landlord, they just don't want to deal with it anymore. Period.

The Lease Option. A lease option agreement can be a great tool to acquire a home under certain circumstances. I call a Lease Option an "incomplete sale" or a "hanging sale" because you take possession of the property now intending to own the home forever. But the title change won't officially occur until an event happens–a triggering event. Therefore the sale hangs there, incomplete, under the terms of the agreement, waiting for the triggering event to occur.

The landlord is called a Landlord/Seller, and the renter is called Renter/Buyer. This strategy can be a really good one when the buyer has cash in hand but does not have all the other parts needed to apply for a mortgage with a bank. The bank needs evidence of things like good credit, tax returns, or solid employment. You may not have those now, but you expect to have those things in short order, further down the road. You also need a motivated seller/landlord who can do this. Remember, the home technically is not sold. So the Landlord/Owner needs to have the financial ability to move into another home, get another mortgage, etc. Many people can buy another home only after they first sell their existing home and pay off their mortgage.

Let's go back to our $2000/month scenario and pencil in a lease option. Remember, in this case, you need to have money in hand. You could lease the property for 60 months, at the rate of $2000/month. You offer to give the seller/landlord $30,000 for the right to purchase the home for $200,000 at any point over the next 60 months. And to do that, you just need to inform the seller you wish to open escrow with 30 days' notice. The $30,000 becomes the down payment, and it pretty much becomes a conventional sale at that point. In addition to the $30,000 for the option, part of your monthly payment could be added to the down payment. For example, $500/month out of the $2000 could be applied to the down payment. You could always sweeten the deal by offering a large security deposit. This could be applied to the monthly rent in the event of an emergency, applied to the down payment, or even given back at closing.

The home price in both cases is fixed. You are living in the home, part of your monthly payment is paying down principal, and you have five years to get your finances in order.

The downside to the lease option is that you have the risk of the seller/landlord not paying the bank and putting the home into financial distress. You have the risk that if your financial situation does not improve and you don't exercise the option, you will lose the $30,000. While these risks have not been eliminated, with a financial plan in place, these risks have been reduced tremendously. Plus, you can always build into the arrangements that the seller/landlord verifies to you his or her payment to the bank each month.

Other Agreements. There are numerous ways to acquire a home. They are typically called "contracts of sale." The key to all of them is a solid understanding of your financial plan, especially your income and expenses and your financial snapshot. Take the leap of faith and become a homeowner. Become a part of your community and the society you live in.

"Get out and Stay out!"

CHAPTER 10

Asset Protection Strategies

Level the Playing Field - Sins of the Past

I do not, nor does this book, recommend that you avoid or escape your responsibilities. If you have financial obligations, you need to deal with them. You might think you can get away with doing nothing, but thinking that way will only make things worse. You need to own up to your responsibilities because it's the right thing to do. It's simple, really. There's good, and there's evil in everyone. This book is teaching you to do the right thing— the godly thing to do.

On the other hand, we believe that you don't have to be bullied and forced into this by the government or anyone else. You've probably had enough of that already.

If you have followed this workbook, you should have a solid understanding of your cash flow and a very good idea of how much you can afford to pay for your outstanding obligations. It's in the best interest of everyone not to be overburdened. Too many times people try to do too much of the right thing, and it gets them into trouble. The system, for the most part, is set up to take as much money as they possibly can get, upfront, monthly, weekly… they do not care. Most of the time, it's some form of artificial intelligence system calling the shots anyway. AI just doesn't care. It doesn't care if you succeed or fail. Sometimes, I think that a lot of these existing systems are just designed to keep you down in life rather than allow you to build yourself up and change your life.

Overburdened felons can potentially put everyone at risk because of the potential of resorting back to criminal activity to meet financial obligations. This is a real deal. Today, as I am working on this section of the book, a man located in Odessa, Texas, lost his job and killed a bunch of people. Although we may find out his real motives at some point, my experience tells me that after he lost his job, he started thinking about the rest of his life. He didn't think he had a chance to be anything. He made a wrong left turn, which started a gunfight that left 7 people dead and 22 people injured. I can assure you that the chances of this happening would have been far reduced if he had his finances in order.

Financial stress is a real deal, and it makes crazy people do crazy things. Many times these bureaucracies think too short-sided. They think that getting repaid as soon as possible is the only thing that's important. But on the other side of that transaction is a human being. My suggestion is that felons need breathing room and understanding, especially if they have been in custody for more than 6 months. In the system today, that breathing room currently just does not exist. And the system is set up to start the pressure the moment you become a free man.

On the other hand, you have a moral obligation to be responsible for your responsibilities, and frankly, it is simply the right thing to do. You need to pay your debts to people or entities that you owe. So you are in a bit of a pickle, right? (Wrong.) Know this: your situation doesn't mean you have to be forced to sign an unfavorable installment agreement that you cannot afford. Signing something like that can have long-term, debilitating affects on your life physically and mentally.

So how do you deal with all of this? Two ways. One, know your cash flow by heart, frontward and backward, inside and out. Second, level the playing field. Another name for leveling the playing field is? Drumroll .... *asset protection strategies*.

There are books written on the subject of asset protection, and this chapter is in no way anywhere near all-inclusive. Plus, this is not a one-size-fits-all situation. We would need volumes upon volumes of text to encompass all the possibilities.

The purpose of the chapter is to bring the issues to your awareness and urge you not to stand by idly waiting for some administrative action to be taken against you. Those administrative actions could be as simple as one day you go to your ATM and find your balance at zero. Another surprise could be the company that you work for getting a legal notice to withhold 25% of your salary. Or other surprises could be that your Social Security has been offset by 15% or your house has a new lien attached to it. These are massive attacks and can broadside the best of us, turning important things into EMERGENCIES!

So rather than react by "Creating A's All Over Your Goal Planning List" and "living in the world of emergencies," it's much better to be proactive. Having an asset protection plan in hand before your release really really helps. In many cases, just taking charge of your responsibilities in the eyes of your creator, creditor, or government agency puts you in a much better light. We want to create a strategy that prevents anyone from taking your stuff automatically without your knowledge. And then, because they can't get your things, you can now negotiate a settlement in good faith. So the purpose of the strategy is not to avoid your responsibility. Instead, it so you can negotiate without having to be under pressure.

Who are some of these potential creditors that you may have to deal with upon exiting jail or prison? The Internal Revenue Service (IRS), Child Support, the Department of Education, commercial creditors, e.g. credit card companies, auto loans and leases, court-ordered probation reports, Franchise Tax Board for Restitution, or Back Taxes. I personally had to deal with back taxes upon being released from prison. I was already in the collection phase, and the tax lien was imminent. Rather than wait for them to come at me, the first thing I did was to get the year in question into compliance by filing a return for that year. Then the tax was calculated. While I could not afford to pay it, I was upfront and gave them my best efforts. God rewarded me with an easy-to-pay installment agreement that put me back in good standing with the IRS. The liens were released, and that automatically improved my credit score.

Realize that any property held in your own name is fair game. Real Estate, savings, and checking... everything that was on the asset list you created. The exception, in most cases, is pensions and individual retirement accounts. This is because they are not titled in your name. They are titled in the name of another (The Pension Trust or The Retirement Trust) for your benefit. Just like in prison, money earned or money your family has sent is placed in a trust account for your benefit. That's why, during your incarceration, your creditors can not attach your trust funds. Once you are released and funds are taken out of your EBT card, they become fair game.

Most importantly, don't get lazy. Be responsible, take charge of your obligations, and reach out. If it's Child Support, reach out to your wife (or the baby's momma) involving family support. Step up to the plate and discuss it. Let them know you are willing to help and that you care. You care about your children and want to be the parent you're supposed to be. Then start thinking about the Internal Revenue Service, State Taxation, Restitution, and The Department of Education. You can save commercial creditors for last. In all cases, look at your cash flow and promise only what you can deliver. Let them work it out. If you can only afford $5/month for restitution, then only offer $5. Even though you think that's not enough, and it probably isn't, but only pay what you can afford.

At the same time, here are some of the strategies you can employ to reduce your exposure. This is not a cure. This is not a comprehensive list by any means. Some attorneys specialize in asset protection.

Here are the strategies:
- Have your property held by another natural person, e.g., a close and dear personal friend that you absolutely trust with your life. This is another reason why it is so important to develop and nurture relationships while in cus-

tody. You have the time, you have the focus. Pick up the phone, and if you can't, send letters. But build tight relationships.

- Have your property held by another unnatural person. Certain Trusts can provide a layer of protection as long as you do not have direct control over the assets. This is a job typically for a skilled Estate Planning Attorney. Keep in mind that these trusts are very special and require an experienced attorney familiar with asset protection strategies. No matter which trust or entity used, the important thing to remember if you want protection is that you cannot have total control and domain over the asset.

- Establish a Limited Liability Company "LLC" or other business entity where you do not have direct control over the assets. A couple of things to consider here. Just creating an LLC or Corporation does not instantly provide protection. You need to treat this entity as a business and not as a personal checking account. You should not be buying food and clothing and going out to the movies with this account. If you use it as a personal account, they can and will bust through the entity and take your stuff. A business needs to be treated like a business. Only business expenses should be paid through this account. Consider that the first step in protecting the assets of the LLC in which you are managing or operating. The second step is to change control by adding another member to LLC, and having all the decisions require a unanimous vote. The nuts and bolts of a limited liability company are written in a document called an Operating Agreement. These agreements can be very creative and very effective.

CHAPTER 11

Arming Yourself for the Casino

If you are this far in the book, you've studied hard. You've been serious. Yep, you're in custody, but that doesn't mean you can't take a break and have some fun. What I'm about to teach you was something that was taught to me by some very wealthy, sophisticated businessmen. This happened after I lost $10,000 one night in the Tropicana Casino in Atlantic City, New Jersey. That was not fun. In fact, it was so depressing that, even though I was taken by helicopter from Fairchild Republic Airport in Farmingdale, Long Island, NY and then a Limousine to the Casino, and I had a $1500 dinner compliments of the Casino, and a suite for the night— IT STILL WAS DEPRESSING!

It really pissed me off. Anyway, these guys who enjoyed playing Blackjack taught me the system that I'm going to share. Of course they taught the system to me only AFTER I lost the money!

In the late 1970s and early 1980s, when you lived in New York, you either flew to Las Vegas or the Caribbean to gamble at a casino. That's not the case today. Almost anywhere in the United States, you are a few hours away from a casino. Now, I realize that you are probably going to go gamble no matter what I say. So rather than to tell you to stay away or never gamble, let me arm you with a strategy that has allowed me to get back my $10,000. Not all at once. I do confess it was $8000 one night and many $2500 to $3000 nights. This system will give you the ability, or should I say a chance, to actually come back home with some MONEY. Also, I know that access to playing cards is usually, if not almost always, available in custody. Everyone gets so bored that this is something you can do every day and keep tabs on how much you have won or lost. Before we get started, I want to share something else with you.

Do you remember when we discussed earlier about comparing credit card debt with the wise use of leverage? There is a big difference between gambling and Investing. When you gamble, you are specifically taking odds against you. There are 9 horses in the race, 8 of those horses are going to lose, and only 1 will win. So the chances are not in your favor. But with investing, things can be more in your favor.

For this example, we will use the Stock Market. In order to be a publicly-traded stock, the registration process is rigorous, and the accounting must be presented to the public. Accounting for the company is done quarterly. In most cases, the company is either manufacturing, owns rights to, or has a license to do something very profitable. About the only thing that the stock market and gambling have in common is that you don't know what going to happen tomorrow. If you think about that, that's just about everything in life. It takes years of understanding to invest. But it is certainly worth the time and effort if you like that kind of thing. Playing blackjack has nothing to do with investing. It has nothing to do with making a living. This is about having fun. When you go to the casino, you should have a fighting chance to break even or even come home with some money.

The system is not about picking the right cards. I will show you exactly what card to take or not to take under every possible situation. On the following pages, I have included the rules of the game and the exact cards to pick. But this is nothing special and this information is not secret. You can buy it on a poker size card in every casino gift shop— "The Best Odds Cards to Pull in Blackjack." Also, we did not have chips in prison. We tried M&Ms, but everyone wanted to eat them. Cookies were too messy. We didn't have enough checker pieces. But we did have a lot of mustard, mayo, ketchup, and salad dressing packs in our lunch sacks. We accumulated them and made sure the guards knew we weren't trying to make Pruno out of the ketchup packs. The packs worked just fine as casino chips.

This system is a money management system based on the simple fact that "Luck Comes In Streaks." People win all the time at the blackjack table, but they don't come home with the money. Why? Because they do not know when to leave the table. This system teaches you when to leave the table. That is why it is so successful.

About 3 months before my EPRD date, I asked my neighbor who has been down 23 plus years, if he would like to learn how to play the game of blackjack and a very special money management system. When I left prison, he was up $90,000! We played with 2 full decks of cards. He played with $2000 each session (20 mayo packs) or (40 mustard packs). Mayo was valued at $100, and mustard was valued at $50. You can make the mayo and mustard any denomination you want. It doesn't matter. What does matter is following the system and documenting the results nightly. You need 20 units per session minimum. If you lose 20 units, you are done for the night. It's over— you lost. The next day is the next day. We played about half an hour to an hour before chow time as well as about half an hour after chow when we returned back to our dorm. Dorm 4, "the old guys' dorm" in Jamestown, was one of the few dorms that had only bottom bunks. So we used the top bunk on my rack as the card table. There was one dealer (who for the most part was me) and three players. Some nights we only had two other players and some nights only one other player head to head against the dealer.

Blackjack is a very common game, and most people know the rules. But if you don't, here they are.

BLACKJACK RULES

Blackjack Card Values

You need to know the card values to understand how to play 21. Cards 2-10 are worth the value of the number on the face of the card. Numbered cards are worth the corresponding number indicated on the card. Face cards (those with pictures on them) are worth 10, except for the Ace, which is worth 1 or 11. A picture combined with an Ace is blackjack (10+11 = a value of 21).

21 Card Game Explained

The most important blackjack rule is simple: beat the dealer's hand without going over 21. If you get 21 points exactly on the deal, that is called a "blackjack." When you're dealt a blackjack 21, it's customary to pay out 3:2 or 2:1. That means you win $300 for every $200 bet at 3:2, or $200 for every $100 bet at 2:1. Clearly. 2:1 is a better payout. In the Dorm, we paid out 2:1. Some casinos have moved this down to 6:5 or 7:5; however, this means you'll get considerably less money over the long haul. A game that pays 1:1 on any kind of a blackjack is usually not even worth looking at.

Whether you're at a land-based casino, cruise ship, or playing online blackjack, the gambling table is always laid out the same way. When you learn how to play 21 (see https://www.blackjack.org/resources/how-to-play-blackjack-online/), you will find each player has his or her own assigned betting area, laid out on the table for each seat position. The playing area includes a space for his/her cards, a betting area, and possibly an insurance field or location for a double down bet. The dealer, likewise, has a designated area for his or her cards, plus a "shoe" containing at least one deck of cards. A shoe is a box that might include an automated shuffler to randomly distribute a card each time the dealer removes one for the deal. Obviously, we did not have an automatic shuffle machine. What we did have was two sets of two decks. While the dealer was dealing the hands, one of the other players shuffled the cards. That way, we could keep the game moving and not have to stop to shuffle.

Traditional land-based casinos, as well as online blackjack casinos, will use between one and as many as eight decks per game. This helps to thwart those who might be counting cards or are considered "advantage" players who know how to manipulate blackjack rules. While counting cards is legal, a casino will ban anyone it considers to be too highly-skilled and capable of imposing an advantage over the house in one or more casino games. Again, all of this really doesn't concern you because the system your learning has nothing to do with counting cards.

Counting cards essentially is the act of tracking the number of high and low-value cards used to better predict a more likely outcome on a particular hand. You can count all the cards you want, but if you do not know when to leave the table, you won't be heading to the cashier's booth to cash out.

By the way, here's a great thing to do: stand by the cashier's window and see how many people really cash out. You will see thousands of people playing, and you will only see 10 or more cashing out. Sad, very sad, but you don't need to concern yourself. If you follow the easy instructions to the letter, your chances of coming home with money are highly likely.

Now that you know the basic tools of the game, it's time to examine how to play. The blackjack rules assign numerical blackjack card values to every card.

Blackjack Basic Table Rules

When you play the house, you play against the casino, which is represented by the dealer. The dealer deals one card up or face down to each player, from left to right, with the last card going to the house's hand. The dealer will then deal one card facing up to each player and then the house.

After the initial deal, the blackjack rules indicate that the dealer will ask each player in succession if he/she needs one or more cards. As the player, you can ask for one or more cards—called a "hit"—until you either go over 21, or you think you have the best possible hand. Once you have all the cards you need, you "stay" or "stand"—meaning you signal to the dealer that you don't want any more cards. Each successive player then decides whether to hit or stand.

After all the players have completed their hands or gone bust, the dealer reveals his or her hand. Depending on the cards in the dealer's hand, the blackjack rules at the table will dictate whether the dealer will hit or stand.

Once the dealer's final hand is established, all players who did not go bust compare their scores to the dealer's hand. Those who beat the dealer win, while the rest lose—unless they tied, which is called a "push." A push is considered "no action" and refunds the player's bet. Some casinos, though, might declare a push to be either a loss or a win for the player. The casino's 21 rules should say exactly how they handle such ties with players.

Blackjack Rules For Dealers

To understand how to beat the house, you need to know how the dealer is affected by the casino's 21 rules for dealers. The dealer mainly plays by the same strict set of casino rules at all times. Those blackjack rules are designed to protect the house advantage over the long term by ensuring the dealer plays a simple, mistake-free game every time.

Over the long run, that means the house will earn a profit—no matter how many card players try to beat it over time.

In fact, the more people try to beat the house, the more the house will win from those who are gambling without abiding by a similarly strict set of blackjack rules. When it's the dealer's turn to reveal the hole card (which is the card dealt face-down), the dealer will use the same rules every time to determine his or her next move. If the card total is 16 points or lower, the dealer will always draw another card from the deck. The dealer will continue drawing cards from the deck until the house hand has at least 17 points, or until it goes bust by going over 21. If the dealer has 17 points off the deal without an

Ace, most blackjack rules say the dealer will stand, even if a 21 player has a higher total.

The dealer also might have a soft 17 hand, which is one that includes an Ace and any other cards whose combined value totals six points. Both land-based casinos and online blackjack casinos who support live dealer blackjack require dealers to take at least one more card when the dealer has a soft 17 showing. The dealer will continue taking more cards—until the house's hand either becomes a hard 17 or higher, or the hand goes over 21 and goes bust.

Blackjack Bonus Payouts

When playing blackjack, as soon as a player is dealt a winning hand, the house pays out immediately. The only time the player will not receive an immediate payout on a blackjack 21 hand is when the dealer's face-up card is an Ace, or any card worth 10 points. The reason for this is that if the dealer also holds a blackjack hand, then the round is considered to be a draw or a "push."

In the case of a push, the player gets his or her bet back, and the game is declared "no action." Some casinos, though, will boost their advantage by giving the house an automatic win whenever it has a blackjack 21 score, even if the player does, too. These games are the most unfavorable to the player and should be avoided. That makes it very important to ensure you know the house blackjack rules before you begin gambling.

Blackjack Table Limits

The table limits in blackjack vary from one casino to the next—both in land-based and online gambling casinos. The table limits usually start at a minimum of $5, while online casinos even offer hands of only $1. Each casino might also have a maximum betting amount, which can range anywhere from $50 to $50,000. Those casino tables are "high-limit" tables that typically have just one or two players going against the house. Most 21 gaming tables accommodate up to six players, but the cost of high-limit tables generally limits the number of players. All of this is really just for your information. You will be playing for mustard and mayo packs, and it's all good.

Blackjack Insurance — A Side Bet

Insurance essentially is a bet on whether or not the dealer has 21 right off of the deal, and requires players to lay half their initial wagers. If the dealer has 21, the house will pay the insurance bets at 2:1. That payoff will wipe out the loss from the initial wager. If the dealer does have 21, the player will lose the initial bet, but will receive a 1:1 payout on their insurance amount, and so they will receive that same amount back. If both have 21, most blackjack rules say that is a push.

Some casino's 21 rules, though, give ties to the dealer when it comes to a blackjack. In most cases, though, a push results in the player getting back his or her wager. It's as if the hand never happened. If the dealer does not have blackjack, anyone who bought insurance will lose that amount, regardless of how the rest of the hand plays out.

HIT OR STAND?

Based on their dealt cards, players can either choose to request another card with a "hit." They also can decline any additional cards with a "stand."

It is important to note that players have a variety of options to choose from after their first two cards are dealt. The decisions they make should take into account the cards held by other players at the table, as well as the dealer. In most cases, a player normally stands when the point value of their cards is between 16 and 21.

Do Dealers Hit on a Soft 17?

If a dealer has less than 17, they must continue drawing cards until they reach 17 or above, without going over 21. Once the dealer reaches a score of 17 or more, he/she will then stand. The dealer's score is then compared to the score of each player. If the scores of the player and the dealer are equal, the player receives their original bet back, and this is a push.

Should the dealer bust or go over 21 at any point, all the players at the table will win and receive a 1:1 payout. Any player who had blackjack would have already been paid out at least 3:2 during the round or as much as 2:1.

Blackjack Surrender Rules

Depending on the casino, some will let players cut their losses by surrendering half their bets after the initial deal. An *early surrender* allows the player to surrender when a 10 or face card is drawn without checking the hole-card for blackjack.

That could be preferable if the dealer is showing a particularly strong hand, like an Ace. A *late surrender* allows the player to surrender after checking the hole-card, but before the dealer reveals his or her hand. Many players view the early surrender as more favorable, especially if the dealer is showing an Ace.

Blackjack Splitting Rules

If the dealer deals you two cards with the same blackjack card value, the rules say you may "split" them into two separate hands by placing another bet equal to your initial wager. For example, virtually all players of 21 will split a pair of Aces by placing an additional bet to create two potentially winning hands. After receiving two more cards, the player determines whether to hit or stand with each of the two hands he or she now has.

Sometimes, after splitting the cards on an initial deal, some casinos will allow a "re-split if the player winds up with another hand with two cards of the same numerical or face value. Depending on the cards dealt, splitting your cards can double your chances of hitting a blackjack. Splitting cards can also at least double your potential winnings from the same initial hand dealt. Highly skilled players will assess their card values versus the card showing in the dealer's hand to determine when splitting cards is the wise play. Most will not split a pair of cards worth 20 points, for example, while all will split a pair of Aces.

Blackjack Double Down Rules

Another popular play that could double your potential winnings—and losses—on a particular hand is the double down. The double down allows you to double your wager after the initial bet, but you only get one more card. If that one additional card is enough to beat the dealer's eventual hand, you win double the amount of cash. If it does not beat the dealer's hand, you could wind up losing double your initial bet.

Many skilled players use a strict system based on statistical probability to determine the ideal times to double down. As with splitting cards, that assessment includes what the dealer is showing off the deal, plus other cards that might already have gone into play. The number of decks used also affects the ideal strategy for playing 21 and considering when to double down on your bet.

The common blackjack rules that actually tilt the game in the player's favor (assuming perfect strategy is used) are as follows:

- Single deck or two decks used
- Early or late surrender allowed
- Unlimited doubling allowed
- Players can re-split aces and draw to them
- Player wins automatically if they draw six cards without busting

What Difference Does The Number Of Decks Make In Blackjack?

To the average blackjack player who is not counting cards, it makes very little difference in terms of expected return and house edge. Card counters want as few decks as possible to simplify their counts, however.

Players place their bet into the box in order to be dealt in.

The game of 21 starts with players pushing their bets into the respective betting box or circle located in front of them. Usually, gaming chips with clearly marked values are used to represent cash wagers.

Once all players have placed their bets, the dealer will then instruct them that no more bets can be placed—except under special circumstances.

The dealer will deal a card from the shuffled shoe to the first player on their left and will then continue towards their right until all players have been dealt a card.

At this point, each player has some options on what to do—which affects their wagers for the entire hand. Here's a closer look at them.

Basic Strategy

(taken from https://www.cs.bu.edu/~hwxi/academic/courses/CS320/Spring02/assignments/06/basic-strategy.html)

The **most important** thing to learn about playing blackjack, and I cannot stress this enough, is to use the basic strategy. The basic strategy was created by using a computer simulation of millions of blackjack hands. One of the first blackjack simulations was done by Julian Braun of IBM.

Basically, these computer simulations showed the mathematical probability of improving the blackjack hand or beating the dealer by using a certain playing strategy. In other words, telling the blackjack player what action he or she should take (hit, split, double-down, etc.) for each and every possible card combination.

It is important to remember that nearly all basic strategy rules are indisputable in the long run. The finite nature of mathematical science dictates that a particular playing decision, based on the player's cards and the dealer's exposed card, will yield a predictable outcome after millions of hands of play.

It is imperative as a blackjack player to learn this basic strategy. By using it, you will eliminate the normal 5 or so percent advantage the casino has over the unskilled player. With this basic strategy, the house advantage is only about 0.5 percent! That is less than a 1 percent disadvantage to the player. This is why blackjack can be one of the most profitable games to play in a casino.

The basic strategy varies according to the type of playing conditions that you are exposed to, namely, how many decks that are in the shoe you are playing. Below I have listed the basic strategy rules for single-deck games and for multiple-deck shoes. Another fact that I must stress is to play **exactly** the way listed below. Do NOT alter your play based on some hunch that you have or by a perceived idea that you *always* lose when you split eights, for example. You may think that you lose more often than you win in certain basic strategy situations, but this is NOT the case over the long run. The only time you should vary from basic strategy is under certain circumstances where you are counting cards. But always remember, even the most skilled card counter will still use basic strategy for the vast majority of his or her playing decisions.

So I urge you to study the rules below and practice them until they do not require any thought on your part. There are many inexpensive blackjack games that you can buy for your iPhone, and several free ones are available as well. Regardless of how you practice, whether it be simply with a deck of cards or on your phone, you MUST learn basic strategy to have any hope of being a consistent winner at the blackjack tables.

The charts below should be self-explanatory. On the left-hand column is the total of the cards you have in your hand and the proper playing strategy based on the dealers up card.

Single Deck - Basic Strategy

Your Hand	vs	Dealer's Up Card
8		Double on 5 to 6. Otherwise hit.
9		Double on 2 to 6. Otherwise hit.
10		Double on 2 to 9. Otherwise hit.
11		Always double, except when the dealer has a 10
12		Stand on 4 to 6. Otherwise hit.
13 to 16		Stand on 2 to 6. Otherwise hit.
17 to 21		Always stand.
A,2 to A,5		Double on 4 to 6. Otherwise hit.
A,6		Double on 2 to 6. Otherwise hit.

Your Hand vs	Dealer's Up Card
A,7	Double on 3 to 6. Stand on 2,7,8, or A. Hit on 9 or 10.
A,8	Double on 6. Otherwise stand.
A,9	Always stand.
A,A	Always split except when the dealer has a 10
2,2	Split on 3 to 7. Otherwise hit to at least 17
3,3	Split on 4 to 7. Otherwise hit to at least 17
4,4	Same as 8 above.
5,5	Same as 10 above.
6,6	Split on 2 to 6. Otherwise hit.
7,7	Split on 2 to 7. Stand on 10. Otherwise hit.
8,8	Always split except when the dealer has 10
9,9	Split on 2 to 9 except 7. Stand on 7,10 or A.
10,10	Always stand.

The above chart assumes the casino doesn't allow doubling down after pair splitting. If the casino allows doubling down after pair splitting then use the following pair splitting rules.

Your Hand	vs	Dealer's Up Card
2,2		Split on 2 to 7. Otherwise hit.
3,3		Split on 2 to 7. Otherwise hit.
4,4		Split on 4,5 or 6. Otherwise hit.
6,6		Split on 2 to 7. Otherwise hit.
7,7		Split on 2 to 8. Stand on 10. Otherwise hit.

*Preferred Strategy "Luck Comes in Streaks"

Now you know the rules and you know what cards to pick. That's not the big deal. As I said earlier, what cards to pick are no mystery, yet the casinos continue to win and continue to build more casinos. Why? Because people don't know when to quit. The money management system is a big deal because it teaches you when to quit— when to leave the TABLE and cash in and get out of there. If you follow the rules I'm going to give you and pick the cards shown, with just a little luck, you can leave the table with money— sometimes a little and sometimes a lot. Still, it's better than losing.

Try to use the FOUR, SIX, EIGHT DECK - card picks listed below. For whatever reason and I'm not sure why, I've won more money using the money management system with four decks or more. If you have a choice and the cards are available use 4 decks or more.

To keep the game going try to have 4 decks shuffled and ready to go while the dealer is dealing. This way you don't have to wait for the shuffle. If you have two decks of cards, keep one shuffled and the dealer dealing.

You need to create a bank for the dealer and every player needs 20 units. That could be 20 mayo packs. I have nothing against ketchup or mustard, whatever you choose give each player 20 packs representing $100 each or $2000. Make sure the dealer has plenty of whatever pack you are using to be able to pay everyone out. If you run short make one of the other condiments have a value of $500 so you can buy them up.

Ok, here we go:
- Everybody place your bets! Use a mayo pack ($100) and put it on the table near you, then play the hand.
- If you win, let it ride so that your next bet is $200. Then play your hand.
- If you win, you are going to be paid $200 for a total of $400. Take 1 mayo pack back, and only bet $300. Put the $100 back to your bank. Play the hand and win!
- If you win, you are now paid out 3 mayo or $300. This time you add one of those to the bet and take two back to your bank. So your next bet is $400 or 4 mayo packs. You are now playing the hand with a $400 bet.
- If you win, you are paid $400. Add 1 to your bet and take 3 back to your bank. You now have a $500 bet. Play the hand.

☐ If you win, you are paid $500. TAKE All 5 BACK to your bank. You still have a $500 bet.
☐ If you win, you leave all of it on the table for a $1000 bet. Keep playing, taking all of your winnings, until you lose. Then it's over— you leave the table, you cash in, you take the money and run.
☐ You should cash in anytime you get a winning streak of 5 or more hands in a row. If at anytime you lose, you go back to 1 unit (or $100) and start over.

If you did this correctly, here are the results:

1st Bet $100	Win result $200	Let it Ride
2nd Bet $200	Win result $400	Take $100 Back
3rd Bet $300	Win result $600	Take $200 Back
4th Bet $400	Win result $800	Take $300 Back
5th Bet $500	Win result $1000	Take $500 Back
6th Bet $500	Win result $1000	Let it Ride
7th Bet $1000	Win result $1000	Take $1000 Back
8th Bet $1000	Win result $1000	Take $1000 Back
9th Bet $1000	Win result $1000	Take $1000 Back
10th Bet $1000	Win result $1000	Take $1000 Back
11th Bet $1000	Win result $1000	Take $1000 Back

This is a ***$6100 winning streak***

12th **Bet $1000**   **Lose**   **Head to the cashier**

And for those who wondered why I stopped at 11, that's because that's the longest streak I ever had.

Four, Six, Eight Deck - Basic Strategy

For whatever reason, my personal experience using the money management system has been with four decks or more. If given a choice, I highly recommend that you use the chart below.

Your Hand vs	Dealer's Up Card
5 to 8	Always Hit
9	Double on 3 to 6. Otherwise hit.
10	Double on 2 to 9. Hit on 10, A.
11	Double on 2 to 10. Hit on A.
12	Stand on 4 to 6. Otherwise hit.
13	Stand on 2 to 6. Otherwise hit.
14	Stand on 2 to 6. Otherwise hit.
15	Stand on 2 to 6. Otherwise hit.
16	Stand on 2 to 6. Otherwise hit.
17	Always stand.
18	Always stand.
A,2	Double on 5,6. Otherwise hit.
A,3	Double on 5,6. Otherwise hit.
A,4	Double on 4 to 6. Otherwise hit.
A,5	Double on 4 to 6. Otherwise hit.
A,6	Double on 3 to 6. Otherwise hit.
A,7	Double on 3 to 6. Stand on 2,7 or 8. Hit on 9,10 or A.
A,8 to A,10	Always stand.

Your Hand	vs	Dealer's Up Card
A,A		Always split except when the dealer has 10
2,2		Split on 2 to 7, Otherwise hit.
3,3		Split on 2 to 7. Otherwise hit.
4,4		Split on 5,6. Otherwise hit.
5,5		Never split. Treat as 10 above.
6,6		Split on 2 to 6. Otherwise hit.
7,7		Split on 2 to 7. Otherwise hit.
8,8		Always split except when the dealer has 10
9,9		Split on 2 to 6, 8 or 9. Stand on 7, 10, or A.
10,10		Always stand.

CHAPTER 12

Consider a New Life in a New State or Even a New Country

If you had professional credentials, you might want to re-establish them. California has the right to accept or deny any of the professional designations and licenses provided. They are in no way lacking in licensing. They license everything. Because of the volume of licenses they manage, they have canned processing procedures that can give you a much needed second chance. The key to renewing your professional license is disclose... disclose and disclose. Do not try and hide your felony or misdemeanor. Check the box "yes" on the application. Tell them what happened and what you have done to resolve the issue, with a promise of never again. California wants you to work, to pay taxes, to pay license fees, to buy gas, to drink bottled water, and to register your car. This creates lots and lots of money, which feeds the California State Budget. They can also decline your request, so make sure you have a Plan B.

If you decided that you want a cleaner life, but you really don't want to go through months and sometimes years of explaining and defending or apologizing for your mistakes, there are other options. Once you have completed your probation, you are free to move about the country. In fact, you are free to move around the world. America is a beautiful country with every state in the union offering something special. But some states need more labor than others. So why not move to where the jobs are?

The following information can be found at this link: http://ghepublishing.com/jobs

10. TENNESSEE — Powered by a construction hiring spree in one of the hottest real estate markets in the country, the Volunteer State has been adding jobs — real jobs — at a record clip. In May 2018, unemployment dipped below the national average, leading to talk of labor shortages and upward pressure on wages. Is the job growth sustainable? Overall, economic growth in Tennessee is also outpacing the rest of the country, but not by as much as the job market is.

- Year-over-year job growth: 1.95%
- Jobs added: 57,500
- Growth industries: Construction, leisure and hospitality
- Top States Economy rank: No. 5

9. **TEXAS** — Low oil prices threw the Lone Star State's economy for a loop in 2016, but the job market and overall economic growth appear to be making a comeback in the first half of 2017. Hiring is still spotty, with information technology still shedding jobs, and a slowdown in construction hiring to go with a cooling real estate market. After several years as the nation's engine for job growth, unemployment in Texas is above the national average. So while hiring is rebounding, job seekers will face some extra competition.
    - Year-over-year job growth: 2.22%
    - Jobs added: 266,600
    - Growth industries: Mining/oil, professional and business services
    - Top States Economy rank: No. 25

8. **WASHINGTON STATE** — America's Top State for Business in 2017 gets there on the strength of the nation's fastest-growing economy, and that is fueling the job market. The IT sector is humming in Washington, and so are mining and logging, construction and hospitality. But watch out for a slowdown in manufacturing as the state's largest employer, Boeing, sheds jobs. With unemployment closely tracking the national average, job seekers will get a lot of attention here. More important, labor is not in such short supply that employers are curtailing hiring.
    - Year-over-year job growth: 2.35%
    - Jobs added: 76,200
    - Growth industries: Information technology, construction, mining/logging
    - Top States Economy rank: No. 3

7. **GEORGIA** — The Peach State's economy was especially slow to recover from the Great Recession, but lately it has been making up for lost time. That is good news for job seekers. Led by a surge in mining and logging and a recovering construction sector, Georgia is hiring again. Unemployment remains stuck above the national average. But with an economy growing nearly twice as fast as the nation's, prospects for the state — and its workers — are strong.
- Year-over-year job growth: 2.36%
- Jobs added: 103,100
- Growth industries: Mining/logging, construction, finance
- Top States Economy rank: No. 1

A FELON'S GUIDE TO FINANCIAL RECOVERY • 265

6. **OREGON—** Industrious Oregonians have caught the wave of economic growth surging in the Pacific Northwest. Unemployment is well below the national average, and companies are still hiring at a steady clip. The Beaver State is traditionally a resource-based economy, including logging and mining, both of which are solidly in expansion mode. But the real push has been in construction, with double-digit job growth in a red hot housing market.
   - Year-over-year job growth: 2.37%
   - Jobs added: 43,300
   - Growth industries: Construction, mining/logging
   - Top States Economy rank: No.10 (tied with Nevada)

5. **COLORADO** — The transformation of Colorado's economy has been something to behold for several years now, making the Centennial State a perennial competitor in our overall rankings. But with the lowest unemployment rate in the nation at a mere 2.3 percent in May, the hiring boom may be reaching its limits. Consistent with the state's move to a more tech-based economy, employment in mining and logging has fallen sharply from its peak in 2014. Manufacturing has been flat at best for more than a year. But in the service sector, job growth, while steady, is only moderate. That may have something to do with the high wages that a workforce in short supply can demand.

- Year-over-year job growth: 2.4%
- Jobs added: 62,000
- Growth industries: Services, leisure and hospitality
- Top States Economy rank: No.13

A FELON'S GUIDE TO FINANCIAL RECOVERY • 267

4. **IDAHO** — It may be hidden in terms of national attention, but the Gem State's economy is strong. The state is aggressively pursuing international investment to make up for its flagging mining and logging sector. Unemployment is at its lowest level in decades, with particular growth in health care to serve an aging population. The West is the fastest-growing region in the country. Idaho lags some of its neighbors there, but the hiring surge is no small potatoes.
   - Year-over-year job growth: 2.43%
   - Jobs added: 16,800
   - Growth industries: Health care, finance
   - Top States Economy rank: No. 8

3. **NEVADA** — The Great Recession badly tarnished the Silver State's economy, but lately it's on a roll. First, tourism in Las Vegas rebounded as consumer confidence rose. Now the real boom has arrived. It is in construction, with double-digit job growth in the past year. Nevada's housing market was among the nation's hardest hit in the 2008 collapse. Today it is one of the healthiest in the country, with home prices appreciating nearly 9% last year. Builders are rushing to cash in on that. That means jobs. It's a win-win.

- Year-over-year job growth: 2.71%
- Jobs added: 35,000
- Growth industries: Construction, professional and business services
- Top States Economy rank: No.10 (tied with Oregon)

2. **FLORIDA** — The Sunshine State is another place where the clouds from the Great Recession have lifted and the future looks bright. The housing market, so decimated in the collapse, has come roaring back, bringing construction employment along with it. Of course, Florida has a long history of overbuilding, leading to an often wrenching boom-bust cycle in the real estate market. Fortunately, other sectors in the Florida job market are growing as well, including the important service sector and even manufacturing.
   - Year-over-year job growth: 2.73%
   - Jobs added: 228,000
   - Growth industries: Construction, services
   - Top States Economy rank: No. 2

1. **UTAH** — The job market in the Beehive State has been in an absolute sweet spot, with perhaps the most vibrant tech scene in the nation. But Utah is also seeing solid gains in construction consistent with its neighbors in the West, thanks to one of the healthiest housing markets in the country. The state could be hitting some headwinds, however. Hiring in the IT sector has slowed markedly in the first half of 2017, following its meteoric rise the past two years. Meanwhile, the broader service sector is still adding jobs, helping to make up for big declines in mining.
   - Year-over-year job growth: 3.28%
   - Jobs added: 46,600
   - Growth industries: Services, construction
   - Top States Economy rank: No. 4

If moving to another state isn't the answer, consider moving out of the country. Mexico, parts of Europe, South America, and Thailand are all worth a serious look. They have a much lower cost of living than in the United States. It would be a fresh start, new friends, new people, and a new culture. In most countries, there are no felon restrictions for visitation, but there can be restrictions for residency. I suggest you research the country very well. But I can tell you this, if you're not looking for trouble, they want you there. Columbia, Costa Rica, Portugal, Thailand, Vietnam... they all want you there. They want your American knowledge and experience. It's a new life, a clean life, and a fresh start.

CHAPTER 13

In California Expect the Unexpected

Do they really want you to rehabilitate in California, or are they really interested in job security? Sometimes I wonder about what is really going on here. The Governor's budget for 2017 proposes total expenditures of **$11.3 billion** for the California Department of Corrections and Rehabilitation. 11,300,000,000 dollars! That's a lot of money! Most of it is payroll and benefits, with a lot of mouths to feed. What happens if one day everyone decides not to commit crime? Who's happy and who's sad?

Here's what I would recommend: Do not commit parole violations. Do not commit criminal acts. Don't even get a speeding ticket. Avoid driving. And never drink and drive. Don't associate with criminals. Build an honest life for yourself. 11.3 Billion Dollars!?!

Many of the inmates I met over my 3.5 years in custody, in my opinion, did not belong there. I found one-third of them uneducated. One third were dealing with substance abuse. And one third were dealing with less serious violent crimes. I did meet several murderers convicted of their crimes when they were young adults— 18 and 19 years old. They worked their way down from Level IV custody to Level 1 non-violent, but now it was 20 or 30 years later. The uneducated need to be educated. The substance abusers need long-term programs. The low-end violent group needs phycologists and anger management programs. There are reasons why we have prisons— for those who commit serious crimes no question. But California, in particular, has more people in custody than anywhere in the world. So remember, like everything else in California, incarceration is big business.

A Few Parting Shots

Faith is not something to be understood intellectually but rather to be appreciated from experience.

Don't get caught up with the Prison or Jail House BS. Try and stay away from prison and jail politics if you can. Remember that you are not alone, God is with you morning, noon, and night. He's patient and has never given up on you. Join a prayer call or Bible study group. If asked who do you roll with, say "The Christians," even if you're not. Go to church, go to the offered religious services, and stay out of trouble.

Affirm your faith in yourself: All Day Long, Pray, Pray, Pray

I believe that I am very important in God's eyes.

I believe that I can return no matter how far I've strayed.

I believe that I have the inner strength to change.

I believe that I can become truly devoted and close to God.

This word is for you. You, who are questioning friendships and your current circumstances... you, who have seen a glimpse of the dangerous grounds that come with an unhealthy relationship.

- ☐ Maybe it's a co-worker that's causing you to ethically slip?
- ☐ Maybe it's a jealous gossiper in your circle?
- ☐ Maybe it's a relative that has proven disloyal?

The Scriptures say,

Blessed is the one who does not walk in step with the wicked or stand in the way that sinners take or sit in the company of mockers, but whose delight is in the law of the Lord, and who meditates on His law day and night. That person is like a tree planted by streams of water, which yields its fruit in season and whose leaf does not wither— whatever they do prospers. — Psalm 1:1-3

Love all, trust a few, do wrong to none. Learn to close some doors. And keep your distance from toxic people and damaging circumstances — not because of pride or arrogance but simply because they take up too much space, time, and energy. They will lead you away from God's presence fast. Cling to trustworthy people. Walk in life-giving places that add value to your God-given dreams. You must remember humility — Know your place and know your space. Keep in mind that you may not give people access to your heart, but even the toxic ones deserve access to your love as a believer. Give, give, and give it away — as Jesus did. Your love isn't just a one-way street — for the people who meet your needs. Make sure you encourage and help others to be successful too. Even if they have proven to be unworthy of your help.

To conclude, sadly, it is rare to find people who remind you of your value in the Lord and how God truly sees you after you believe in Him. It can become a daunting task trying to find people willing to help you navigate through the challenges of life. They are rare, and they are precious. If you know of one— be it your best friend, your neighbor, your co-worker, your team leader, your manager, your spouse, parents, or friends— deeply appreciate them even as you end the workweek. Find a way to be generous to them with a gift, your time, your energy, and the effort to show them your love — find a way to pray for them today.

What could have been/should have been/might have been if you did it right but didn't. Forget it. "Time travel is still a theory."

Just accept the fact that in life, things often fall apart; most good things, no matter how strong they seem at first, will fall apart eventually. Brooding over possibilities that could have been and should have been is not something very wise to do while in custody. You are not in charge.

If you can't change it, why think about it?

Think about it as a part of life, but really convince your mind that it is. Regret will eat you up alive, and it could only be present if YOU are actually not present. Stay in the NOW. The now is the only place things are happening. Always be aware of your surroundings.

Making excuses instead of decisions?

At certain points in life, you just cannot stall things. Decisions that seem tough, painful, and even unjust have to be taken for the sake of your own well-being.

Survival instincts will often dictate that you stall things and live in the sun for a while longer. But biting the bullet and taking important decisions at crucial times will make life a bit brighter, even though you won't see it then and there.

The worst thing you can do is to refuse to accept your mistakes. One of the many ways to undo that is by being decisive.

If you could just stop and perceive your thoughts. You give yourself excuses all the TIME! There is not one thing right now that you can't do. If you look at it firmly that way, you only lack decisiveness and dedication.

Don't let your mind play games with you. The only thing your mind wants is to be safe. The key to success is feeling uncomfortable in every sphere in life.

Be Careful of Relationship situations that shrink you

Let's face it. When it comes to relationships, we all have spent time belittling ourselves. We need to learn to adjust, adapt, and be flexible in a relationship. We all have a fundamental human need to be loved and to conform.

We don't want to push people away from our lives. When you're in a toxic relationship, most of the time, the toxicity is not from what the person does to you directly. It is from the amount of shrinkage you undergo to fit and conform to the relationship. Have you ever thought about that?

You restrict yourself from everything your partner "thinks" you shouldn't do, until you are no longer yourself.

Take jealousy, for example. If your partner is really a jealous freak, and you want him or her to feel "safe" with you, then you would need to stop talking to men/women to the point where you no longer socialize. In the end, it will make you so miserable that even the partner notices your misery (even if they don't know why). The situation is a lose-lose for both of you.

Beware of old lies that you still cling to. People change, and you change too. So your notions about both of those things— others and yourself— should undergo a change.

Just like a caterpillar becoming a butterfly, so you need to let go of your obsolete beliefs that don't hold anymore. Be free.

Forget the idea that you have to be perfectly fine all the time. There are good days and bad days. People can keep their life together sometimes and sometimes they can't.

Breakdowns are a necessary catharsis to help you see things from a better perspective. You will see your mistakes, and that will help you work on them better. It is okay to be alone, to be unhappy, to grieve the loss of a loved one, to be ill. What is not okay is giving up.

To persevere is the greatest human virtue. Striving to become a better version of ourselves is all we can do, and the best we can do.

Conclusion

It has been an honor to write this book. This book is for you. Give yourself the chance you need to succeed. Remember, "You are wherever your thoughts are. Make sure your thoughts are where you want to be."

Be anxious for nothing, be worried for nothing, be careful for nothing. But in all things with prayer and supplication with thanksgiving, let your request be made known to God. And the peace of God which surpasses all understanding will guard your heart and mind.

God Bless You!

Robert Barth

Money and the Mind?

The findings below come from researchers at the National University of Singapore's Social Service Research Centre. They studied almost 200 low-income people who unexpectedly had portions of their long-running mortgage, utility, and municipal debts paid down by a charity.

Researchers tested participants before and after their windfalls on their ability to spot matches and mismatches. The recipients were also tested for generalized anxiety disorder and their ability to make more beneficial financial decisions.

The results show that getting rid of debt doesn't just unburden finances, it takes a weight off the mind that clears up cognitive functioning, lessens anxiety, and improves impulse control.

The study found:
- Average error rates in the cognitive function tests fell to 4% after the debt was paid down, compared to a 17% error rate beforehand.

- The proportion of participants showing generalized anxiety disorders went from 78% to 53% after the debt relief.
- Numbers of people showing so-called "present bias," which favors instant gratification, dropped to 33% from 44%, a sign that their impulse control had improved.

"Because debt impairs psychological functioning and decision-making, it would be extremely challenging for even the motivated and talented to escape poverty."

— Dr. Ong Qiyan, National University of Singapore

Of course, the experiment played out on the other side of the globe and involved a very small number of people. But the findings are in line with previous research in the U.S. on the psychological toll of living in poverty.

When people live in "chronic scarcity" — meaning they lack sufficient money, housing and food to thrive — their brains become overtaxed because they're coping with **emergency after emergency**, research by the nonprofit consulting firm ideas42 found. That in turn can diminish self-control and harm people's ability "to evaluate options and make high-quality decisions," wrote ideas42. "In short, scarcity makes us less insightful, less forward-thinking, and less controlled," the study concluded.

Many Americans are well-acquainted with the stress that financial uncertainty can create. As the nation faces $1.5 trillion in outstanding student debt, a third of students in a survey last year said their student loan bills were a major source of stress. One man said he and his wife would cry the day they paid their last student loan bill. Debt can also affect your dating prospects. Three quarters of people in one survey said credit-card debts would be a turn-off in a potential mate.

Researchers said the Singapore study was another look at so-called "bandwidth taxes," which are part of the reason some people stayed mired in poverty. "The demands of daily life under scarcity create 'bandwidth taxes' that sap mental resources, impairing cognitive ability and causing counterproductive behavior which perpetuates poverty," the researchers wrote in the study, which was published in the Proceedings of the National Academy of Sciences of the United States of America.

One way to less the bandwidth taxes? Consolidate debt to simplify the pay-off experience, researchers suggested.

America has its own stories about overjoyed debtors who say they have a whole new view of life after their creditors were suddenly satisfied. Last year, Fifth Third Bank said it would pay the approximately $150,000 in student loans of a Chicago single mother with a nursing job.

Afterwards, 30-year-old Jasmin Ford told ABC News,"I just imagine being able to spend more time physically with my family, not having to hustle, having mental freedom and with that, some spiritual freedom. I can open myself to more experiences, opportunities and just be able to sit and be with my thoughts and be able to pursue what it is I came to do."

(*article from https://www.msn.com/en-us/money/personalfinance/getting-rid-of-debt-may-actually-make-your-brain-work-better/ar-BBVoheY?ocid=spartandhp)

The 30 Day Chart!

Day 1	$1
Day 2	$2
Day 3	$4
Day 4	$8
Day 5	$16
Day 6	$32
Day 7	$64
Day 8	$128
Day 9	$256
Day 10	$512
Day 11	$1024
Day 12	$2048
Day 13	$4096
Day 14	$8192
Day 15	$16,384
Day 16	$32,768
Day 17	$65,536
Day 18	$131,072
Day 19	$262,144
Day 20	$524,288
Day 21	$1,048,576
Day 22	$2,097,152
Day 23	$4,194,304
Day 24	$8,388,608
Day 25	$16,777,216
Day 26	$33,554,432
Day 27	$67,108,864
Day 28	$134,217,728
Day 29	$268,435,456
Day 30	$536,870,912

Over a Half a *Billion* Dollars !

GHE Planning For Life

God-Health-Everything Else

ABOUT THE AUTHOR

Educational and Business Background
Robert E. Barth, Author
Managing Member

Robert E. Barth is 67 years young and a Managing Member of GHE Publishing LLC, a publishing and life planning company located in Clovis, California, in the Heart of the Central Valley.

Robert was born in New York, graduated from Plainedge High School in 1970, and attended college at the State University of New York with a Major in Business Administration. His father Joe was a supermarket manager for Waldbaums Supermarket in Merrick, New York. Joe always wanted Robert to work with him, join the strong meat cutters union, and become a butcher. Robert had other plans— he was on a mission to be in his own business from the age of 17. Robert never completed all those college courses. He started a company without any money. With a pencil, paper, a car belonging to his girlfriend (soon to be wife), and a lot of heart, he followed his passion.

In 1972, RDS Photo Inc. was born. RDS Photo was a photo film processing company. Picking up unprocessed film from camera stores, drug stores, stationery stores, and discount stores, the company would have the film processed by a third party. RDS would then re-price and mark-up the photo packages and return the negatives and pictures back to the store for their customers, giving the store a cut in the process.

It was a revolutionary idea at the time— being a photo processing middle man. The company posted signs in New York City in the 70s and 80s. The signs were in yellow, black, and red, stating, "LEAVE YOUR FILM HERE - KODAK FILM DEVELOPED AND PRINTED, SAVE UP TO 50%." Starting from 1972 with just a pad and pencil, Mr. Barth built that business from scratch. He sold it in 1986. It had over 500 active dealers/customers, with 10 daily routes covering Long Island, Brooklyn, Queens, parts of upstate New York, and Manhattan. In addition to the routes, Mr. Barth built and operated his own photo processing laboratory in Oceanside, NY, and managed 6 Long Island retail locations called Photo Discount Outlet Stores. Robert was told by his peers that he was crazy to think that film processing would become a thing of the past in years to come. That did not stop him from selling the business in 1986 and retiring to Hawaii for several years with his wife, Marianne.

In late 1989 he returned to the mainland of California to help his older brother Harry get through law school. At the same time, he began educating himself and learned how to become a financial advisor.

In 1990, Mr. Barth and his wife (6 months pregnant) moved to Laguna Niguel, California, where he returned to school. There he attended the College for Financial Planning's CFP Professional Education Program. At the same time, he applied to Saddleback College in Mission Viejo to complete his degree in Business and Communications. He successfully completed the Certified Financial Planning program in 1991, which became the starting point for a long and successful career in the financial services industry as a Certified Financial Planner. In 1993 he obtained his Associate of Arts in Business with a Major in Accounting from Saddleback College. He would go on to earn his Bachelor of Science degree in the year 2000.

Although Robert is no longer practicing as a Certified Financial Planner, his 20+ year career gave him the honor and privilege of providing financial counseling and advice to a very exclusive, affluent group. That group included: active and retired National Hockey League players and agents, retired National Football League players, Burger King franchisees, Jack in The Box franchisees, Ford dealership owners, physicians, dentists, surgeons, sportswriters, newspaper executives, and other highly compensated executives.

Robert has now changed his focus to helping those who are much more in need of building their wealth and living a balanced life.

The following former designations, experience, and education information is being provided for disclosure purposes only. Mr Barth is no longer practicing as a Certified Financial Planner. He is now a Life Coach or Life Planner.

Education
Plainedge High School, Graduated 1970
State University of New York Farmingdale Partial Term, 1972
College For Financial Planning, CFP Certification 1991
Irvine University College of Law, Completed Contracts and Torts 1992
Saddleback College, AA Accounting and Business 1993
University of Advanced Research, Bachelor of Science, Real Estate

Former Licenses
California Licensed Real Estate Broker
California Licensed Life and Health Insurance
Registered Securities, Series 7, 63, 24, 27
Completed California Examination for Certified Public Accountants

Former Associations
The International Board of Standard for Certified Financial Planners
The International Association of Financial Planners
National Society of Accountants
The Registry of Financial Planning Practitioners
The International Association of Registered Financial Planners
The Institute for Certified Financial Planners
National Association of Realtors
Member of Orange County Multiple Listing Service

Skills and Experience
Real Estate experience which encompasses both residential and commercial acquisitions and sales.
Buying and selling small companies.
As a Manufacturer, Wholesaler, and Retailer.
Raising capital for small companies.

Authored the book : *Get Out and Stay Our - A Felons Guide to Financial Recovery*

Proficient in the disciplines of Personal Financial Planning Specifically the integration of Cash Flow Planning, Risk Management, Asset Protection, State and Federal Income Tax Planning, Investment Planning, Retirement Planning, Education Planning and Estate Planning.

Has a knack for taking a relatively new concept or product and bringing it to market.

Presented seminars and educational workshops all over much of the United States and England.

Appeared on both radio and television

Contact

You may contact GHE Publishing at the following addresses:

General Information:
info@ghepublishing.com

To schedule seminars:
seminars@ghepublishing.com

Robert Barth:
rbarth@ghepublishing.com

To place bulk orders of this book:
bulkorders@ghepublishing.com